I0762554

MORE PLANTS

For Berry and Zach.
Our future is in your hands.

MORE PLANTS

30-minute plant-based meals

Henry Firth
& Ian Theasby

CONT

NTS

A BIT ABOUT BOSH!

Nearly 10 years ago, we started BOSH! with one simple mission: to help more people eat more plants. Back then, recipes for good, plant-rich dishes were often hard to find. Supermarkets were behind the curve, the internet was full of confusing advice, and cookbooks often didn't show us how to cook the food we wanted to eat. So we got onto it.

We set ourselves four ambitious goals: to create a digital recipe platform people would love; write a bestselling cookbook; host a TV show; and launch our own range of products into supermarkets. Within five years, we'd achieved all four.

At the time, we were living and working together, bouncing between our houses in London. We wrote recipes and filmed them during the day, edited them at night, built a business, attended events, made connections, and shared everything on social media. It was crazy, intense, and totally brilliant. Those memories will last a lifetime. We partied hard, worked harder, and cooked even harder still. We built something we're immensely proud of in the process: BOSH! A food brand that has reached many millions of people and encouraged just as many to eat more plants.

But along the way, amid the intense pace, we lost our balance. Even though our work mission remained the same and we were still eating loads of "healthy" home-cooked meals, we didn't feel great—too much sugar, too much alcohol, not enough sleep. We were working flat out, and we weren't thriving. Then, when we both turned 40, and became dads, something clicked, and everything changed. We had less time, more responsibility, and a whole new reason to think long term.

So we got to work. We stripped everything back. We reexamined how we ate, moved, and lived. At the core of it all was our *Flavor for Life* philosophy; the belief that eating more plants, packed with flavor and variety, is the easiest way to feel sharper, stronger, and healthier. We created meals that made us feel energized, satisfied, and genuinely excited to eat. The result? We feel better than we have in years. We've lost weight, built muscle, gained energy, and feel like we'd turned the clock back 20 years. We now track, measure, and set ambitious, health-focused goals. The work has worked. Henry is in the shape of his life, doing triathlons, and Ian's running ultra marathons for fun!

This book distills what we've learned over the years. It's packed with quick, vibrant recipes celebrating fresh, real ingredients, and big flavors. Every recipe is full of plant-rich goodness, with most taking around 30 minutes to cook. You'll also spot that each one comes with a plant points figure (see pp16–17), which is a simple way of counting the number of different plants in a dish, from fruit and vegetables to beans and grains. The goal is to eat 30 different plants a week, a number based on solid nutritional research. This may sound like a lot, but once you get going, and with the help of the recipes in this book, it's a doddle.

You don't have to change everything overnight. Start with one meal, one day, one recipe. Use what you've got. Cook what you enjoy. And build up from there.

Now, let's eat more plants...

Henry and Ian x

Eating more plants is one of the simplest and most powerful things you can do for your health. When we say "plant-rich food," we don't mean boring salads or bland steamed vegetables. That's not the BOSH! way, and it's not what this book is about. We're talking about nutritious, satisfying meals full of color, texture, and flavor. The kind of food that makes you feel good and gives your body what it needs to thrive.

WHY MORE PLANTS?

Your gut, brain, heart, blood, and bones all benefit from eating more plants. It's not just about getting more protein, vitamins, and minerals into your diet; it's vital to give your body the variety of nutrients it needs to feel energized, stay strong, and function at its best.

Just as important as volume is diversity. Plants provide a variety of nutrients your body needs—from fiber and phytonutrients to antioxidants and prebiotics—with each one supporting your overall health, including a strong immune system and diverse gut microbiome.

Recent studies recommend we eat 30 different plants per week, and fruit, vegetables, beans, grains, nuts, seeds, herbs, and spices all count. You may be wondering where this figure originates. It corresponds to the findings of one of the largest gut health studies ever carried out: the independently funded American Gut Project, which started in 2012. Researchers based at UC San Diego's School of Medicine and the Earth Microbiome Project found that individuals who consumed 30 or more different plant foods each week had significantly more diverse gut microbiomes than those who ate fewer than ten.

A diverse gut microbiome has been linked to improved health outcomes across the board, including reduced inflammation, improved metabolic health, more efficient nutrient absorption, and a stronger immune system. Since gut microbial diversity tends to decrease as we get older (believed to be linked to some of the chronic diseases associated with aging, including obesity, type 2 diabetes, Alzheimer's, and Parkinson's disease), it becomes even more important to redress any imbalances by eating a diverse plant-based diet. This is further supported by a study that looked at the gut microbiome of two groups of healthy people in China: one group aged between 90–99 and a second group, who were over 100 years old. It found that both groups had a better gut microbiome than younger adults who ate less diverse diets. These findings were confirmed by similar studies carried out in Japan and Italy.

That's why variety matters and explains why we've packed so many different plants into the recipes in this book. Think abundance, in the best possible way. We don't want you to cut things out. We want you to get greedy and add more in. When it comes to plants, more is more.

The best part? You don't have to be perfect. There's no need to track every bite or measure every portion. We've made it simple by building variety into the recipes, and we've even counted the plant points for you. So all you need to do is cook, eat, and enjoy.

GO FOR COLOR

Eating a variety of different-colored plants guarantees a diverse intake of a range of vitamins, minerals, and phytonutrients, each with its own set of health benefits. Each color, even if it's the same type of fruit or vegetable, will add to your plant points count.

Red (tomatoes, strawberries, red peppers, watermelon, red grapes): rich in the antioxidant lycopene and vitamin C, which support heart health and immunity.

Orange & yellow (oranges, peaches, nectarines, mangoes, sweet potatoes, orange peppers, carrots): rich in beta carotene, which your body converts to vitamin A for healthy skin, vision, and immune support.

Green (green tea, spinach, leafy greens, avocados, broccoli): rich in iron, folate, and vitamin K. Iron helps carry oxygen in the blood and supports both energy levels and brain function. Folate supports cell function and tissue growth, while vitamin K is important for bones and blood clotting.

Blue & purple (blueberries, black grapes, blackberries, purple cabbage, eggplants): rich in antioxidants that support brain and memory function and may reduce the risk of heart disease.

Your body works hard every day: thinking, moving, and recovering. Food keeps it running smoothly, and eating a nutritious diet, based on a wide variety of plants, provides your body with what it needs. Plant foods are made up of the same building blocks as most other types of food: energy (calories), protein, carbohydrates (including fiber), and fats. Understanding these helps explain why variety matters and why plants do such a good job of fueling your body. No tracking, no logging, just a few basics and simple healthy habits will carry you a long way.

WHAT YOUR BODY NEEDS

Calories

These are units of energy found in all foods and drinks—your body uses calories to think, move, grow, recover, and stay alive. Every cell in your body needs calories to function, so getting enough of them matters. If weight loss is your goal, creating a calorie deficit can help, but that doesn't mean going hungry, eating a restricted diet, or obsessing over numbers. The good news is that fiber-rich, plant-based foods can help you feel fuller with fewer calories.

The focus in this book is on feeling full and energized, using whole, plant-rich foods that nourish and sustain. Fiber, protein, healthy fats, and slow-burning carbs work together to steady your blood sugar, reduce cravings, and keep your energy levels up.

These recipes are built to fuel you properly and support your goals. Eating well should feel good, so instead of counting calories, we count plant points (see p17).

Fiber

Fiber does more than keep you regular. It feeds the good bacteria in your gut, helps manage blood sugar, supports healthy cholesterol levels, and reduces the risk of heart disease, type 2 diabetes, and some types of cancer, plus fiber satisfies the appetite.

There are two main types: soluble fiber dissolves in water to form a gel-like substance, which slows digestion, helps control blood sugar levels, reduces cholesterol, and expands in the gut to help you feel fuller for longer; and insoluble fiber, which doesn't dissolve, and keeps everything moving through your digestive system, making stools softer and easier to pass, helping to reduce problems, such as constipation, hemorrhoids (piles), and diverticular disease.

Many plant foods offer both types of fiber: beans, lentils, whole grains, fruits, vegetables, nuts, and seeds are all great sources. These foods are also rich in prebiotics—the nutrients that feed your gut microbes.

Most people don't get enough fiber. Only 4 percent of adults manage to eat the recommended 1oz (30g) of fiber a day. Hitting that target will do wonders for your gut.

Protein

Helping to build muscle and support your immune system, protein plays a key role in recovery after injury or illness. You don't need to eat meat, fish, or dairy to get enough—plants can give you everything you need, if you eat a good variety across the week. Tofu, tempeh, lentils, beans, peas, nuts, seeds, and whole grains, like quinoa, are all excellent sources of plant protein.

Protein is made up of amino acids, which your body cannot make, so you need to get them from your diet. Some foods, like soy and quinoa, are complete proteins, containing all 20 essential amino acids, while others contain only some, but by eating a variety of plant foods across the day and week, you will easily cover the full set your body needs. Many recipes in this book contain over 1oz (20g) of protein per serving, making it simple to feel strong and energized.

Carbohydrates

Your body's main source of energy, carbs fuel your brain, muscles, and every cell in your body, making this food group especially important if you are very active.

Carbs are found in a wide range of plant foods, including fruits, vegetables, beans, lentils, whole grains, nuts, and seeds. Yet not all carbs are created equal. Refined carbs, such as white bread, pastries, and sugary snacks, are digested quickly and can cause a spike in blood sugar levels, followed by a dip in energy. A diet high in refined carbs is linked to insulin resistance, high blood pressure, and heart disease. At the other end of the scale, slow-burning carbs—including whole grains, beans, lentils, root vegetables, and fruit—are broken down more gradually, giving you steady amounts of energy, keeping you full for longer, and supporting a healthy gut microbiome.

Carbs provide fiber (see pp10–11), vitamins, and minerals, which is why plant-rich sources are so beneficial. Around half of your daily energy should ideally come from carbohydrate-rich foods, so focusing on whole, unprocessed plants is the best way to keep your body fueled, satisfied, and in balance.

Good gut health

Fermented foods are packed with beneficial bacteria that can support your gut health, digestion, and immune system. These microbes, known as probiotics, help balance the gut microbiome, which plays a key role in everything, from mood and energy production to reduced inflammation and nutrient absorption.

Adding just a small number of fermented foods to your meals each day can contribute to improved health. Think kimchi, sauerkraut, miso, tempeh, plant-based yogurt or kefir, and kombucha—these foods bring flavor and a welcome boost to your gut.

You don't need much, just regular, small amounts as part of your daily diet: try a spoonful of kimchi on top of your stir-fry, or have a glass of kombucha in the afternoon. Your gut will thank you.

kMix

A note on supplements

As part of our journey to maximize our personal health spans, we both take a carefully curated mix of supplements that we feel genuinely help. For us, it's not just about adding years to life but adding life to those years.

Supplements aren't essential, and neither are they a substitute for a healthy diet, but they can be a smart choice, especially for those on a plant-based diet. Prevention is better than cure, and a few well-chosen additions can help fill any nutritional gaps.

A good-quality multivitamin is a solid place to start. A vitamin B12 supplement is vital if you're eating mostly, or entirely, plant-based foods. Vitamin D is another key nutrient: in fact, experts in the UK recommend that all adults and children over four take a 10 microgram supplement from October to March, when there isn't enough sunlight for the body to make enough naturally. We also take omega-3 and magnesium, which support energy, recovery, sleep, and mood. If you are vegan, check that the vitamin D and omega-3 supplements do not contain any animal- or fish-derived ingredients.

Healthy fats

Fats often get a bad rap, but they're essential for good health. Fats help your body absorb vitamins and phytochemicals, support hormone production, power your brain, and keep you feeling full and satisfied. They also play a key role in managing inflammation and protecting your heart. Studies show that the absorption of phytochemicals like lycopene and beta carotene is significantly increased when foods like tomatoes, green vegetables, and carrots are served with fat. One study carried out at Ohio State University found that lycopene absorption was over four times higher when a tomato salsa was eaten alongside an avocado, a source of healthy fat. A similar study found that the bioavailability of carotenoids was significantly increased when a dressing was added. So adding an oil-based dressing to your salad not only enhances taste, it makes it even more nutritious.

Alongside avocado, other plant-rich sources of healthy fats include olive oil, nuts, seeds, and tahini. These foods not only add flavor and texture to meals, but they also help your body thrive.

Don't be afraid of fat. You need it to feel energized, stay sharp, and support long-term health. A little fat at each meal goes a long way to supporting you.

Vitamins & minerals

Working in partnership with the macronutrients, protein, carbohydrates, and fat, are vitamins and minerals. These micronutrients work together to support overall health (see Go for Color on page 9), providing antioxidant protection as well as looking after our skin, bones, internal organs, and vision. By eating a diet based on a wide range of plant foods, you can ensure you are getting a good range of vitamins and minerals, including vitamin B12 and calcium.

Broccoli, kale, almonds, and fortified plant milks provide calcium, which, together with vitamin D, is essential for healthy bones. Calcium helps build and maintain strong, dense bones when you are young and reduces the risk of osteoporosis (brittle bones) later in life.

Vitamin B12 is important for energy production, brain health, and red blood cell formation. Since it's usually found in animal products, the vitamin can be more difficult to get through a plant-based diet. The good news is it's simple to stay topped off with fortified foods, such as yeast extract, plant-based milks, nutritional yeast, and some breakfast cereals, as well as by taking a food supplement (see left).

Every plant you eat—fruits, vegetables, grains, pulses, nuts, seeds, fungi, herbs, and spices—contributes to the overall number of points you eat on a weekly basis.

WHAT ARE PLANT POINTS?

Plant points help you eat more plants without overthinking or too much planning. There is no diet. No tracking app. Simply remember that one plant generally equals 1 plant point (see right).

The goal is to eat 30 different plants across the week. It may sound like a lot, but it adds up fast. A bowl of oatmeal with a berry and mixed seed topping could give you up to 7 points. A lentil curry with sweet potato, spinach, garlic, and ginger provides even more. Before you know it, you're there...

Why does it matter? Because your gut loves variety. Different types of fiber feed different microbes in the gut (see pp10–11). This helps everything from concentration and digestion to sleep and mood. It's kind of like magic, without the spell.

To make things easy, we've counted the plant points in each recipe for you. No spreadsheet is needed. Just cook, eat, and let the points look after themselves; simple, effective, and helpful.

Bear in mind that not all ingredients that contain plants count toward your points total. Plant points are about celebrating whole, natural ingredients, so some foods don't make the list: foods like white bread, white pasta, and white rice don't bring much to the table in terms of fiber or nutrients, so they don't earn a point. While they aren't on the complete no list, if you can opt for whole grain or whole wheat, when possible, then all the better. When it comes to chips, cookies, and other ultra-processed snacks, even if they technically contain a small amount of plant matter, they don't contribute to your points count. Focus on variety from fresh, unprocessed whole foods, and you'll naturally hit the target.

HOW TO CALCULATE PLANT POINTS

Fruits & vegetables
1 point for each type of fruit and vegetable. Even two different colors of the same fruit or vegetables contribute separate plant points. Fresh, frozen, and canned all count.

Beans & pulses
1 point for each type of bean or lentil, including tofu, tempeh, and hummus. Check out fresh, frozen, dried, and canned.

Nuts & seeds
1 point for each different type of nut and seed. Ground and whole count.

Whole grains
1 point for each different type of whole grain, including whole wheat pasta, oats, quinoa, brown rice, whole wheat noodles, and spelt.

Herbs & spices
¼ point for each herb and spice (fresh and dried).

Other plant-based foods
1 point for 70 percent cocoa plain chocolate.
¼ point for olive oil, coffee, and tea.

Thirty plants may sound like a stretch. But once you get into the habit of eating plant-based meals regularly, it happens almost without trying. Here are a few suggestions to help you boost your weekly plant point count.

HOW TO HIT 30 PLANTS A WEEK

Pump up the plant points

- Sprinkle seeds on everything. Check out our seed blends on page 208–209.
- Use our plant-boosting sauces and condiments to drizzle over soups, salads, stews, and noodles—basically anything you fancy (see pp216–218).
- Finish a pasta, grain, or noodle dish with one of our Meaty Toppers (see pp220–223) or Crispy Tofu (see p224).
- Add a simple side salad to most meals.
- Grate or finely chop extra vegetables into sauces, stews, or stir-fries.

Cook once, eat twice
Roast a tray of vegetables, cook a pot of grains, whip up a punchy dressing, or prep a quick bean salad. These all keep well and will help give a plant-points boost to lunches, dinners, and more. See our BISH BATCH BOSH! recipes (p150–181) to set you on the right path.

Upgrade your base
Swap white rice for wild rice, brown rice, or quinoa. Try whole wheat or plant-based pasta instead of white. Toss lentils or beans into your tomato sauce. More flavor, more nutrients, and more plants.

Double up your herbs & spices
Herbs and spices are an easy win: fresh parsley, mint, basil, cilantro, and more; fresh and dried spices, such as fresh ginger, whole dried spices, and ground mixed spice blends all add flavor and variety, and help reduce the amount of salt you need, too.

Use your freezer
Frozen spinach, peas, sweet corn, edamame, and berries are quick, colorful, and always ready to add extra plant points to your meals.

Mix up your beans
One can of mixed beans equals up to four plants in one hit. Simple.

Snack on plants
Nuts, energy balls, fruit (fresh and dried), crudités, granola (see p29), snack bars (see p195)—the list of plant-rich snacks is huge!

The goal is variety, not perfection
Some weeks you'll hit 30; others you won't. That's fine. More color, more texture, more flavor = more plants. That's the win.

Take your pick from these daily menus for extra plant points; super protein-packed; easy, speedy; and batch-cooked meals to pull from the fridge or freezer, and enjoy right away.

MORE PLANTS DAILY

SUPER PLANT-POINT DAY

These dishes are all bursting with plants, guaranteeing that you reach an impressive plant point count in one day!

HARISSA POTATO BREAKFAST HASH

see p38

ULTIMATE SUPER-FOOD SALAD

see p85

SMOKY BBQ PULLED OYSTER MUSHROOM TACOS

see p114

PEAR, GINGER & BLUEBERRY CRUMBLE

see p200

EASY, SPEEDY DAY

These simple recipes can all be whipped up in a flash.

BLUEBERRY AÇAI POWER SMOOTHIE

see p49

MAKE-AHEAD MISO NOODLE SOUP JARS

see p54

SWEET CHILI TOFU LETTUCE CUPS

see p75

CHOCOLATE BANANA "CAKIES"

see p199

PROTEIN-PACKED DAY

If you ate these 4 recipes in one day, you'd hit a whopping 114g of protein!

PROTEIN-PACKED BREAKFAST PUDDING

see p35

PICKLE BEAN-STUFFED BAKED POTATOES

see p111

PROTEIN-PACKED BLACK DAL

see p156

SILKY CHOCOLATE POTS

see p190

BATCH-COOKED DAY

Stash away these treats in your pantry, fridge, or freezer for a make-ahead feast!

FRUITY NUTTY GRANOLA

see p29

SWEET ROAST TOMATO & CHILI SOUP

see p179

TOFU TIKKA MASALA

see p176

COCONUT & CARDAMOM RICE PUDDING

see p197

These are the plant-based ingredients that we reach for most regularly when cooking the recipes in *MORE PLANTS*. They're not the only ingredients you'll find in this book, but they're the core players that make it easy to create quick, flavor-packed, nutritious meals as well as hit your 30 plant points a week. Think of them as the BOSH! pantry. Stock up when you can, swap for seasonal or local produce, and don't stress if you don't have every single ingredient.

ESSENTIAL INGREDIENTS

Food group	Ingredient
Fruits & vegetables	Apples, artichokes, arugula, avocados, bananas, beets, blueberries, bok choy, broccoli, butternut squash, cabbage (green, white, and red), carrots, cauliflower, celery, cucumber, eggplants, garlic, grapes, green onions, kale, kiwi, leeks, lemons, lettuce (various), limes, mango, mushrooms (fresh and dried), orange, peppers (various colors), pineapple, pomegranate, potatoes, radish, raspberries, snow peas, spinach, strawberries, sweet corn, sweet potatoes, tomatoes (fresh, canned, sun-dried, and paste), Tuscan kale, zucchini.
Freezer favorites	Berries (various), edamame, herbs (cilantro, dill, and basil), mixed vegetables, peas, spinach, sweet corn.
Grains, pulses & legumes	Barley, beans (black, butter, cannellini, chickpeas, kidney), bulgur wheat, couscous (regular, whole wheat, and pearl), lentils (split red, green, black urad), millet, noodles (udon, ramen, soba, preferably whole wheat), oats, pasta (various, preferably whole wheat), pearl barley, polenta, rice (Arborio, basmati, long-grain, short-grain, preferably whole grain), quinoa, spelt, tempeh, tofu (firm, extra-firm, smoked, and silken).

Food group	Ingredient
Nuts, seeds & butters	Almonds, Brazil nuts, cashews, chia seeds, flaxseeds, hazelnuts, hemp seeds, nut butters (peanut, cashew, and almond), peanuts, pecans, pine nuts, pistachios, pumpkin seeds, sesame seeds (black and white), sunflower seeds, walnuts.
Dairy alternatives	Coconut yogurt, plant-based cream, plant-based milk, plant-based plain yogurt.
Oils & fats	Coconut oil, plant-based butter, olive oil, extra-virgin olive oil, good-quality neutral oil, toasted sesame oil.
Herbs & spices	Basil, bay leaf, black pepper, cardamom, chili, chives, cilantro, cinnamon, cumin, dill, fennel seeds, garam masala, garlic granules, ginger, mint, nutmeg, oregano, paprika, parsley, rosemary, sage, smoked paprika, sumac, tarragon, thyme, turmeric, za'atar.
Flavor boosters and condiments	Agave syrup, apple cider vinegar, balsamic vinegar, capers, crispy chili oil, Dijon mustard, harissa paste, hoisin sauce, kimchi, liquid smoke, maple syrup, miso paste (white and brown), nutritional yeast, pickles (cornichons, gherkins, and onions), plain chocolate (70 percent), rice wine vinegar, sauerkraut, sea salt, soy sauce (light and dark), sriracha, stock cubes, tahini, tamari, teriyaki sauce, white wine vinegar, yeast extract.
Pantry extras	Plant-based mayonnaise, roasted red peppers, olives, good-quality vegetable stock, bouillon powder, shredded coconut, raw cacao powder, coconut sugar.
Breakfast & snack staples	Granola (low-sugar, whole food), dried fruit (dates, raisins, apricots, figs), sourdough bread, tortilla wraps (corn, whole wheat), plant-based naan.

Easy, speedy, and delicious! Each chapter in this book will help you pack in more plant points at breakfast, lunch, and dinner. We have a whole chapter of MORE PLANT HACKS to help you maximize on plant points (see pp204–229), but these are some of our best tips to help with speedy cooking and easy meal prep.

MORE PLANTS HACKED

GET ORGANIZED

Keep your pantry, containing dry ingredients, herbs, spices, oils, vinegars, and condiments, arranged with everything you need within easy reach, and those you use most often easily accessible. Clearly label your seasonings, herbs, and spices, adding a use-by date, so you know what's what.

USE PREPREPPED SHORTCUTS

Keep a good stock of cooked grains, canned/jarred beans, and vacuum-packed beets. These ready-to-go ingredients save chopping and cooking time, letting you whip up salads, curries, soups, or stews in minutes without extra fuss or compromising on nutrition and flavor.

FLAVOR READY TO GO

Keep jars of seed mixes (see pp208–209), nooch (aka nutritional yeast) blends (see pp211–212), and drizzles (see pp216–218) on hand. A quick sprinkle or squeeze instantly adds texture, flavor, and extra nutrients to any dish—the hard work is already done.

KNOW YOUR EQUIPMENT

Is your skillet oven safe? Is your saucepan nonstick? Can you heat up your baking sheet/dish on the stove? Make sure you know which pieces of equipment you can use best for each purpose so that when you're cooking, you don't have any surprises and find you've chosen the wrong pan, tray, or dish.

BEFORE YOU START

Before you start cooking, read the recipe all the way through, set out all the equipment you'll need (each recipe comes with a list), and gather your ingredients.

HEAT FOR SPEED

Grilling and air-frying are excellent ways to speed up cooking, caramelization, and creating flavor! Preheat your oven so that by the time you're ready to cook, everything is nice and hot, and good to go.

BATCH IT UP

Set aside time on the weekend or a quiet weeknight to batch cook recipes from our BISH BATCH BOSH! chapter (see pp150–181). These recipes are cooked lower and slower so the cooking time sometimes exceeds 30 minutes—we figure it's worth it when we are saving you cooking time during the week. All dishes marked BC and/or FR (see right) can be batch cooked and frozen, so you have something tasty on hand when you need it.

EASY STORAGE

Keep a good stock of storage containers handy so you can stash batch-cooked meals and leftovers in the fridge and freezer. Label batch-cooked dishes before storing, so you know how long they will keep for and can easily identify any mysterious frozen containers.

MORE PLANTS KEY

At the top of every recipe in this book, you'll find a small box of nutritional information and kcals per portion (see example, right), along with blue, yellow, and orange icons, where appropriate. Here's what that info means...

PER PORTION:

- 8 PLANT POINTS
- 32g PROTEIN
- 429 kcal

- **PLANT POINTS**

Remember that plant diversity is key! We've counted up the plant points per portion for every dish. Take a look at page 17 to see how we calculate plant points.

- **PROTEIN**

The protein per portion is given in grams. This count includes the protein content of each recipe's key elements, but not optional extras (like an optional side of brown rice). You can bump up the protein count by adding some of our MORE PLANT HACKS (see pp204–229).

- **kcal**

Calories per portion are given in "kcal"—this includes the servings and extras where quantities are given, but not optional extras or ingredients without quantities.

FREEZER-FRIENDLY These recipes all freeze well and can be stored in the freezer to defrost, heat up, and enjoy later.

BATCH COOK These recipes work well cooked in bulk—so you can get ahead on prep and stock up your fridge, freezer, or pantry with tasty treats for future you.

AIR FRYER-FRIENDLY These recipes can be cooked in the air fryer to make your prep and cook times super speedy.

BREA
& BRU

KFAST
NCH

FRUITY NUTTY GRANOLA

PER PORTION:
- 6.5 PLANT POINTS
- 10g PROTEIN
- 390 kcal

Makes about 10 servings

1½ cups (150g) mixed unsalted nuts
2¾ cups (250g) old-fashioned rolled oats
1¼ cups (150g) mixed seeds
2 tsp ground cinnamon
pinch of sea salt
½ cup (125ml) maple (or agave) syrup
6 tbsp (90ml) olive oil (or melted coconut oil)
1 tsp vanilla extract (optional)
⅓ cup(50g) raisins
⅓ cup(50g) dried cranberries
⅓ cup (50g) dried apricots
plant-based milk or yogurt, to serve

Crispy, golden granola packed with nuts, seeds, and dried fruit, gently spiced with cinnamon and naturally sweetened; it's the perfect make-ahead breakfast with milk or plant-based yogurt. It's also great as an after-work snack, but that can be our little secret.

Before you start: line 2 large baking sheets with parchment paper. Preheat the oven to 350°F (180°C).

Mix dry ingredients. Roughly chop the nuts and add to a large bowl with the oats, seeds, cinnamon, and salt. Stir to combine.

Add wet ingredients. Pour in the maple syrup, olive oil, and vanilla, if using, and mix until the dry ingredients are well coated.

Bake granola. Spread evenly over 2 lined baking sheets. Bake for 30 minutes, stirring halfway, and swapping the sheets around, until golden and crisp.

Add fruit. Remove the baking sheets from the oven and let cool completely. Stir through the dried fruit once cool.

Serve and store. Serve with plant-based milk or yogurt. Transfer to a large airtight jar or container—the granola will keep for up to 2 weeks stored at room temperature.

ZACHY'S BANANA BREAKFAST BOWL

PER PORTION:
- **4.5 PLANT POINTS**
- **8g PROTEIN**
- **356 kcal**

Serves 2

4 bananas, plus extra to serve (optional)
2 tbsp nut butter, such as peanut, almond, or cashew
1 tbsp vanilla extract
¼–½ cup (60–125ml) plant-based milk (amount depends on size of bananas)

To serve
2 tbsp Fruity Nutty Granola (see p29, optional)
handful of berries (blueberries and raspberries work well)
1 tbsp pomegranate seeds
1 tsp maple (or agave) syrup
Brain Power seed blend (see p209), to serve (optional)

Ian's son, Zach, absolutely loves bananas and can't get enough of this. No surprise really, it's like eating ice cream for breakfast! We hope you love it as much as Zach does.

Before you start: you will need a high-speed blender.

The night before. Peel and roughly chop the bananas, then freeze them overnight in a lidded freezer container.

In the morning. Add the frozen bananas, nut butter, vanilla, and plant-based milk to a blender. Blend until you have a super smooth, thick, and creamy mixture, adding more of the milk, if needed.

Serve. Pour the banana cream into bowls and top with the granola, berries, pomegranate seeds, and a drizzle of maple syrup. Finish with a sprinkling of the seed blend, if using, and serve right away.

FLORENTINE TOFU SCRAMBLE

PER PORTION:
- **4.75 PLANT POINTS**
- **47g PROTEIN**
- **692 kcal**

Serves 2

9½oz (280g) firm tofu
5½oz (150g) silken tofu, including the liquid from the pack
4 tbsp plant-based milk
¼oz (10g) nutritional yeast
1 tsp cornstarch
¼ tsp ground turmeric
pinch each of kala namak (black salt) or regular sea salt and freshly ground black pepper, plus extra to season

For the spinach
2 garlic cloves
2 tbsp plant-based butter, plus extra to serve
3 cups (100g) baby spinach leaves
1 tbsp water

To serve
3 green onions
slices of sourdough bread, preferably whole wheat

A creamy, satisfying scramble using our famous two-tofu technique. Egged-up with kala namak (black salt) and nutritional yeast, it's perfect on sourdough for a wholesome, plant-packed breakfast.

Before you start: you will need a high-speed blender and a medium skillet.

Prep ingredients. Drain and pat dry the firm tofu with paper towels to remove any excess moisture. Slice, peel, or mandoline the tofu very thinly into long strips. Set aside.

Blend silken mix. In a blender, combine the silken tofu (with liquid), plant-based milk, nutritional yeast, cornstarch, turmeric, and a pinch each of salt and pepper, then blend until smooth.

Cook spinach. Peel and grate the garlic. Melt 1 tablespoon of the plant-based butter in a medium skillet over medium heat. Add the garlic and cook for 2 minutes, until fragrant, taking care it doesn't burn. Add the spinach and water and cook for 1 minute, until wilted. Remove from the pan, roughly chop and season with salt and pepper. Put the spinach in a bowl, cover and keep warm until needed.

Cook scramble. Melt the remaining 1 tablespoon of plant-based butter in the same skillet over medium heat. Add the sliced firm tofu and cook for about 2 minutes, stirring gently to prevent it breaking up too much—the tofu will resemble loose scrambled eggs when ready. Turn the heat down to low, pour the blended silken tofu mixture into the pan and gently stir for 3–5 minutes, until scrambled, glossy, and slightly thickened. Taste and season with salt and pepper.

Assemble and serve. Finely slice the green onions. Toast the sourdough and spread each slice with plant-based butter while still warm. Spoon the spinach on the toast, then top with the tofu scramble. Sprinkle over the green onions and add a final twist of black pepper to serve.

PROTEIN-PACKED BREAKFAST PUDDING

PER PORTION:

- **7.5 PLANT POINTS**
- **29g PROTEIN**
- **356 kcal**

Makes about 20 portions

1¾ cup (200g) macadamia nuts
1¼ cup (150g) walnut halves
⅓ cup (50g) Brazil nuts
¾ cup (100g) chia seeds
⅔ cup (100g) flaxseeds
⅔ cup (50g) raw cacao powder
1 tbsp (10g) ground cinnamon
⅓ cup (40g) sunflower lecithin
1⅓ cup (150g) dried berry powder
5½ cups (600g) pea-protein powder (berry flavors work well)
½ cup (100g) creatine monohydrate powder
1 cup (100g) super-greens powder
1 cup (250ml) water or plant-based milk

To serve

mixed berries
nuts and/or seeds of your choice

Inspired by Bryan Johnson and his mission to optimize health and longevity, this is our take on his famous Nutty Pudding—packed with nutrients linked to anti-aging, brain health, and improved metabolic function. This recipe makes enough for 20 portions of breakfast pudding, but you can easily serve it as a drink, too, by adding extra liquid to the mix.

Before you start: you will need a food processor (or high-speed blender) and a 1½–2 quart (1.5–2 liter) container with lid.

Grind nuts and seeds. Chill the nuts and seeds in the fridge for 15 minutes. Working in batches, pulse the macadamia nuts, walnuts, Brazil nuts, chia seeds, and flaxseeds to a fine, dry meal in a food processor, stopping before the mixture turns buttery.

Blend mix. Pour the ground nuts and seeds into a large bowl. Mix in the cacao, cinnamon, lecithin, berry powder, pea protein, creatine, and super-greens until combined.

Store. Decant into a large, labeled jar or container. Cover with the lid and store in a cool, dry place for up to 1 month.

Assemble and serve. Scoop 2¼–2¾oz (70–80g) of the mix per serving into a blender (or a protein shaker). Pour in 1 cup (250ml) water or plant-based milk and blend until smooth. Pour into a bowl and top with berries, nuts and/or seeds of your choice. Alternatively, adjust the thickness with extra liquid, if needed, to serve as a drink. Enjoy!

OVEN-BAKED BEANS

PER PORTION:
- **9 PLANT POINTS**
- **35g PROTEIN**
- **605 kcal**

Serves 2

1 red pepper
3 garlic cloves
5½oz (150g) shiitake mushrooms
7oz (200g) cherry tomatoes
1 x 15.5oz (439g) can cannellini beans, drained
3 tbsp olive oil, divided
½ tsp garlic powder
½ tsp onion powder
1 tsp sweet smoked paprika
½ tsp ground cumin
sea salt and freshly ground black pepper
9½oz (280g) smoked tofu
1 large handful of baby spinach leaves
squeeze of lemon juice

For the baked bean sauce
2 tbsp tomato paste
1 tbsp maple (or agave) syrup
1 tbsp light soy sauce
1 tsp Dijon (or whole grain) mustard
½ tbsp apple cider vinegar
2–3 tbsp water

To serve
slices of sourdough bread, preferably whole wheat
plant-based butter
chives (or parsley)

Yeah, you could buy a can of baked beans, but if you're feeling fancy, this one's for you—they're smoky, oven-baked, and topped with crispy tofu. Sunday morning sorted!

Before you start: you will need a large roasting pan and a large skillet. Preheat the oven to 425°F (220°C).

Prep vegetables. Dice the red pepper, discarding the seedy core. Peel the garlic, leaving the cloves whole. Slice the mushrooms and halve the cherry tomatoes. Add the vegetables to a large roasting pan with the drained cannellini beans, then drizzle over 2 tablespoons of the olive oil and sprinkle with the garlic powder, onion powder, smoked paprika, and cumin. Season with salt and pepper, and toss until everything is combined.

Roast. Cook the vegetables for 20–25 minutes, giving everything a gentle stir halfway through, until the tomatoes are bursting and are thick and jammy.

Make baked bean sauce. Meanwhile, in a bowl, whisk together the tomato paste, maple syrup, soy sauce, mustard, vinegar, and water to make a thick, pourable sauce. Set aside.

Fry tofu. Drain the tofu and pat dry with a paper towel to remove any excess moisture. Tear up the tofu into small chunks. Heat the remaining 1 tablespoon of oil in a large skillet on high heat. Add the tofu and cook for 6–8 minutes, until golden and crispy. Season with salt and pepper and set aside briefly.

Finish beans. Add the baked bean sauce to the roasting pan. Stir until combined and return to the oven for another 5 minutes, until heated through. Remove the pan from the oven, then stir through the spinach while the mixture is still hot to wilt the leaves. Sprinkle over the crispy tofu and add a squeeze of lemon. Taste and season with extra salt and pepper, if needed.

Assemble and serve. Meanwhile, toast the sourdough and spread with the plant-based butter. Spoon the roasted vegetables and beans generously on top and garnish with chopped herbs.

HARISSA POTATO BREAKFAST HASH

PER PORTION:
- **11.5 PLANT POINTS**
- **34g PROTEIN**
- **559 kcal**

Serves 2

9½oz (280g) smoked tofu
3 medium potatoes, such as Yukon Gold (around 10–12oz/ 350–400g total weight)
1 zucchini
1 red pepper
1 small red onion
2 garlic cloves
1 tbsp olive oil
generous pinch of sea salt, plus extra to season
3 cups (100g) baby spinach leaves
1 tbsp harissa paste
1 tsp sweet smoked paprika
1 tsp ground cumin
½ lemon
1 tbsp nutritional yeast
freshly ground black pepper

To serve
slices of avocado
sliced mild red chile
Fresh Green Drizzle (see p216) or All Day Ranch Drizzle (see p217)
parsley or cilantro leaves

A spicy, smoky breakfast hash loaded with crispy smoked tofu, golden potatoes, and vibrant vegetables. It's finished with harissa paste, warming spices, and zippy lemon for a bright, satisfying start to your weekend.

Before you start: you will need a large skillet with lid.

Prep tofu and vegetables. Drain and pat dry the tofu with paper towels to remove any excess moisture, then cut it into ½in(1cm) cubes. Dice the potatoes (no need to peel), zucchini, and pepper, discarding the seedy core, into ½in(1cm) cubes. Peel and finely slice the onion and garlic.

Cook hash. Heat the olive oil in a large skillet over medium heat. Add the potatoes with a generous pinch of salt, cover with the lid, and cook for 8–10 minutes, stirring occasionally, until lightly golden on the outside and starting to soften on the inside. Add the smoked tofu and cook for another 6–8 minutes, until golden. Stir in the onion, zucchini, and pepper and cook for 6–8 minutes, until everything is cooked through and golden brown.

Flavor and finish hash. Add the garlic, spinach, harissa, smoked paprika, and cumin, then squeeze in the juice of ½ lemon. Stir and cook for 1–2 minutes, until the spinach wilts. Add the nutritional yeast, taste and season with extra salt and some pepper, if needed.

Assemble and serve. Top the hash with slices of avocado and chile. Finish with the drizzle of your choice and a sprinkling of herbs. Bring to the table and dig in.

SMOKY SMASHED CHICKPEA BREAKFAST TACOS

PER PORTION:

- **8.75 PLANT POINTS**
- **7g PROTEIN**
- **227 kcal**

Makes 10

For the smashed chickpeas
1 x 15oz (425g) can chickpeas
1 garlic clove
¼ red onion
1½ cups(50g) spinach leaves
¼ cup (10g) parsley leaves
2 tbsp nutritional yeast
1 tsp sweet smoked paprika
1 tsp ground cumin
2 tbsp cornstarch
good pinch each of sea salt and freshly ground black pepper, plus extra to season

For the fresh toppings
3½ oz (100g) cherry tomatoes
¼ red onion
1 lime
1 avocado
1 handful of cilantro leaves

To finish
olive oil, for frying
10 small corn or flour tortillas

To serve
hot sauce or chili oil
Fresh Green Drizzle (see p216)

Crispy, smoky chickpeas pressed into golden tortillas and topped with fresh tomatoes, avocado, and zingy lime. These breakfast tacos are flavor-packed and plant-point heavy, making them a perfect way to start the day.

Before you start: you will need a food processor (or high-speed blender) and a medium, nonstick skillet.

Prep chickpea mixture. Drain and rinse the chickpeas and pat dry with paper towels. Peel and roughly chop the garlic and onion. Roughly chop the spinach and parsley and add to a food processor with the garlic, onion, chickpeas, nutritional yeast, smoked paprika, cumin, cornstarch, and a good pinch each of salt and pepper. Pulse to a thick, coarse paste, scraping down the sides when needed. Don't overblend; the mixture should hold together but still have texture.

Prep fresh toppings. Quarter the cherry tomatoes and very finely dice the onion, then place in a bowl. Halve the lime and cut one half into wedges (set aside for later). Squeeze the juice of ½ lime into the bowl with the tomatoes and onion, and add a pinch of salt. Halve, remove pit and skin, and slice the avocado. Roughly chop the cilantro, if preferred.

Cook tacos. Lightly oil a medium, nonstick skillet and heat over medium-high heat. Put a tortilla on a clean work surface and place 1 heaping tablespoon of the chickpea mixture in the center. Flip the tortilla, chickpea-side down, into the hot pan and press firmly with a burger press or spatula to spread the mixture evenly under the tortilla, and cook for 1–2 minutes, until golden and crisp. Carefully flip the tortilla over and cook the other side for another minute. Remove from the pan and keep warm and soft under a clean dish towel while you cook the remaining tortillas/chickpea mixture.

Assemble and serve. Top each crispy chickpea taco with a few slices of avocado, spoonfuls of the tomato mixture, and a sprinkling of cilantro. Finish with a dash of hot sauce and a spoonful of the green drizzle, then serve with the remaining lime wedges for squeezing over.

GOLDEN MIXED SEED PORRIDGE

PER PORTION:

- **4.75 PLANT POINTS**
- **12g PROTEIN**
- **467 kcal**

Serves 2

1½ cups (125g) old-fashioned rolled oats
3 tbsp Gut Health seed blend (see p209) or 2 tbsp mixed seeds and 1 tbsp ground flaxseeds
1 tbsp unsweetened shredded coconut
½ tbsp coconut sugar
pinch of sea salt
pinch of ground turmeric
1¾ cups (400ml) plant-based milk (or water)

For the berry compote

5½oz (150g) Longevity Berry Mix (see p213) or frozen mixed berries
1 tbsp maple (or agave) syrup
½ tsp ground cinnamon
¼ tsp ground ginger

To serve

coconut yogurt
mixed seeds or nuts
fresh berries

A comforting, creamy porridge packed with gut-friendly seeds and a warming hint of turmeric. Topped with a vibrant, spiced berry compote and creamy coconut yogurt, it makes the perfect start to the day.

Before you start: you will need 2 small saucepans.

Make berry compote. Add the frozen berries, maple syrup, and spices to a small saucepan over medium heat. Cover with the lid and simmer for 10 minutes, stirring occasionally, until the berries defrost and soften completely and the mixture thickens slightly. Set aside until ready to serve.

Make porridge. Meanwhile, add the oats, seed blend, shredded coconut, sugar, salt, turmeric, and plant-based milk to another small saucepan. Bring to a simmer over low heat and cook for 6–8 minutes, stirring regularly, until creamy and thickened. Add a splash more milk if the porridge looks too thick.

Assemble and serve. Spoon the porridge into bowls, then top with a generous spoonful of berry compote, a swirl of coconut yogurt, and a sprinkling of seeds and fresh berries. Enjoy warm.

APPLE CRUMBLE PORRIDGE

PER PORTION:

- 6.75 PLANT POINTS
- 15g PROTEIN
- 661 kcal

Serves 2

1 apple
1 cup (100g) old-fashioned rolled oats
2 tbsp raisins
1 tbsp ground flaxseeds
1 tsp ground cinnamon, plus extra to serve (optional)
½ tsp ground ginger
¼ tsp ground nutmeg
pinch of sea salt
1¾ cups (400ml) plant-based milk (or half milk, half water), plus extra if needed
1 tbsp maple (or agave) syrup, plus extra to serve (optional)
plant-based yogurt (or cream), to serve

For the crumble topping

1 tbsp coconut oil (or plant-based butter)
4 tbsp old-fashioned rolled oats
2 tbsp chopped nuts, such as walnuts or pecans
1 tsp coconut sugar
pinch of ground cinnamon

A cozy breakfast that tastes like dessert. Creamy, spiced porridge topped with crunchy, golden crumble, and a drizzle of maple syrup. Perfect for mornings when you want something a little special.

Before you start: line a large baking sheet with parchment paper. You will need a medium saucepan. Preheat the oven to 425°F (220°C).

Make crumble topping. In a bowl, mix together the coconut oil, oats, chopped nuts, sugar, and cinnamon. Pour onto a lined baking sheet, spread out evenly, and bake for 12 minutes, until golden and crisp.

Make porridge. Peel, core, and finely dice the apple. Add the apple to a medium saucepan with the oats, raisins, ground flaxseeds, spices, salt, and plant-based milk. Simmer gently for 6–8 minutes, stirring occasionally, until thick and creamy, adding more milk, if needed. Stir in the maple syrup, if using, to sweeten.

Assemble and serve. Spoon the porridge into bowls and sprinkle generously with the crumble topping. Add a dollop of yogurt, a dusting of cinnamon, and a drizzle of maple syrup, if you like, before serving.

ALL THE SMOOTHIES

We're big believers in the power of smoothies. They're the easiest way to pack as many plant points in at the start of your day, contributing to your weekly count. That's why we've gone all out with these recipes—your only problem is deciding which one to make first!

GREEN GODDESS SMOOTHIE

PER PORTION:

- **8.25 PLANT POINTS**
- **3.5g PROTEIN**
- **234 kcal**

Serves 2

1 small ripe avocado
4in (10cm) piece of cucumber
2 pitted Medjool dates
1 small, frozen, peeled banana
1 lime
1 cup (250ml) plant-based milk
1 Green Plant Point Cube (see p215) or 1½ cups (30g) baby spinach leaves
1 tbsp ground flaxseeds
½ tsp spirulina powder
1 small handful of mint leaves

Before you start: you will need a high-speed blender.

Prep ingredients. Halve and remove pit from the avocado, and scoop the flesh into a blender. Roughly chop the cucumber and dates.

Blend. Add the frozen banana to the blender. Squeeze in the juice of the lime and add the rest of the ingredients. Blend until smooth and creamy, adding a splash of water, if needed.

Serve. Pour into glasses and serve right away.

kMix

BEET BERRY SMOOTHIE

PER PORTION:

- 5.75 PLANT POINTS
- 10g PROTEIN
- 366 kcal

Serves 1

1 small, frozen, peeled banana
1 orange
1 cup (250ml) plant-based milk
1 small, cooked beet (not in vinegar)
5½oz (150g) Longevity Berry Mix (see p213)
1 tbsp chia seeds
1 tbsp hemp seeds
1 tsp grated fresh ginger
½ scoop of vegan unflavored or vanilla protein powder (optional)

Before you start: you will need a high-speed blender (for powerful blending, see picture!).

Blend. Add the frozen banana to a blender. Squeeze in the juice of the orange and add the rest of the ingredients, including the protein powder, if using. Blend until smooth and creamy, adding a splash of water, if needed.

Serve. Pour into glasses and serve right away.

BERRY BLAST PROTEIN SHAKE

PER PORTION:

- 3 PLANT POINTS
- 32g PROTEIN
- 429 kcal

Serves 1

1 cup (250ml) plant-based milk
7oz (200g) Longevity Berry Mix (see p213)
1 scoop of vegan vanilla protein powder
1 tbsp ground flaxseeds
1 tbsp almond butter
½ tsp ground cinnamon
1 tsp maple (or agave) syrup (optional)

Before you start: you will need a high-speed blender.

Blend. Put all the ingredients in a blender, including the maple syrup, if using. Blend until smooth and creamy, adding a splash of water, if needed.

Serve. Pour into glasses and serve right away.

CHOCOLATE PEANUT BUTTER CUP SHAKE

PER PORTION:
- **3.5 PLANT POINTS**
- **35g PROTEIN**
- **454 kcal**

Serves 1

1 frozen, peeled banana
1 cup (250ml) plant-based milk (or cold water)
1 tbsp raw cacao powder
1 tbsp peanut butter
1 tbsp chia seeds
1 scoop of vegan chocolate or vanilla protein powder
1 tsp vanilla extract
pinch of sea salt

Before you start: you will need a high-speed blender.

Blend. Add the frozen banana to a blender with the rest of the ingredients. Blend until smooth and creamy, adding a splash of water, if needed.

Serve. Pour into glasses and serve right away.

MATCHA PISTACHIO SMOOTHIE

PER PORTION:
- **4.25 PLANT POINTS**
- **24g PROTEIN**
- **506 kcal**

Serves 1

1 frozen, peeled banana
2 tbsp shelled, unsalted pistachios
2 pitted Medjool dates
1 cup (250ml) plant-based milk
1 tbsp hemp seeds
1 tsp matcha powder
½ tsp vanilla extract
½ scoop of vegan unflavored or vanilla protein powder (optional)

Before you start: you will need a high-speed blender.

Prep ingredients. Put the pistachios and dates in a bowl, pour over enough hot water to cover and let soak for around 30 minutes (or overnight).

Blend. Add the frozen banana to a blender. Drain the pistachios and dates and add to the blender with the rest of the ingredients, including the protein powder, if using. Blend until smooth and creamy, adding a splash of water, if needed.

Serve. Pour into glasses and serve right away.

BLUEBERRY AÇAI POWER SMOOTHIE

PER PORTION:
- 6 PLANT POINTS
- 11g PROTEIN
- 428 kcal

Serves 1

1 small banana
1 cup (250ml) plant-based milk
3½oz (100g) frozen unsweetened açai purée (or 1 tbsp açai powder)
3½oz (100g) Longevity Berry Mix (see p213)
3½oz (100g) fresh or frozen blueberries
1 tbsp ground flaxseeds
1 tbsp almond butter
1 tsp lemon juice
few basil or mint leaves

Before you start: you will need a high-speed blender.

Blend. Peel the banana and put it into a blender with the rest of the ingredients. Blend until smooth and creamy, adding a splash of water, if needed.

Serve. Pour into glasses and serve right away.

PEANUT BUTTER, BANANA & DATE SMOOTHIE

PER PORTION:
- 4.5 PLANT POINTS
- 8g PROTEIN
- 445 kcal

Serves 1

1 large, frozen, peeled banana (or use unfrozen)
1 tbsp peanut butter (smooth or crunchy)
2 pitted Medjool dates
1 tbsp old-fashioned rolled oats
1 tsp maca root powder
pinch of ground cinnamon
1 cup (250ml) plant-based milk
few ice cubes
½ scoop of vegan unflavored or vanilla protein powder (optional)

Before you start: you will need a high-speed blender.

Blend. Add the banana to a blender with the rest of the ingredients, including the protein powder, if using. Blend until smooth and creamy, adding a splash of water, if needed.

Serve. Pour into glasses and serve right away.

MEGA MOCHA SMOOTHIE

PER PORTION:
- **4.75 PLANT POINTS**
- **12g PROTEIN**
- **521 kcal**

Serves 1

1 frozen, peeled banana
250ml (1 cup) plant-based milk
1 tsp instant espresso powder (or 1 shot cold espresso)
1 tbsp raw cacao powder
2 tbsp old-fashioned rolled oats
1 tbsp chia seeds
2 tsp maple (or agave) syrup
1–2 pitted Medjool dates
pinch of ground cinnamon
½ scoop of vegan unflavored or vanilla protein powder (optional)

Before you start: you will need a high-speed blender.

Blend. Add the frozen banana to a blender with the rest of the ingredients, including the protein powder, if using. Blend until smooth and creamy, adding a splash of water, if needed.

Serve. Pour into glasses and serve right away.

SPICED CHAI SMOOTHIE

PER PORTION:
- **4.25 PLANT POINTS**
- **8g PROTEIN**
- **310 kcal**

Serves 1

1 frozen, peeled banana
250ml (1 cup) plant-based milk
1 tbsp almond butter
1 tsp maple (or agave) syrup
1 tbsp ground flaxseeds or chia seeds
½ tsp ground cinnamon
¼ tsp ground cardamom
¼ tsp ground ginger
pinch each of ground cloves and nutmeg
few ice cubes (optional)
½ scoop of vegan unflavored or vanilla protein powder (optional)

Before you start: you will need a high-speed blender.

Blend. Add the frozen banana to a blender with the rest of the ingredients, including the protein powder, if using. Blend until smooth and creamy, adding a splash of water, if needed.

Serve. Pour into glasses and serve right away.

PLAN
PACK
LUNC

T-
ED
HES

MAKE-AHEAD MISO NOODLE SOUP JARS

PER PORTION:
- **9.25 PLANT POINTS**
- **42g PROTEIN**
- **745 kcal**

Serves 2

9½oz (280g) smoked firm tofu
1 carrot
2 baby bok choy
3 baby corn
2¼oz (70g) shiitake mushrooms
1 bunch of green onions
1 handful of sugar snap peas
2 in (5 cm) piece of fresh ginger
1 lime
½ cup (150g) white miso
4 tbsp light soy sauce
2 tbsp sesame oil
2 tbsp rice wine vinegar
2 tbsp maple (or agave) syrup
2 x 3½–4oz (100–120g) portions ready-cooked noodles (udon work well, preferably whole wheat)
5oz (140g) kimchi
2½–3 cups (600–700ml) water, to serve

To serve (optional)
crispy onions
roasted unsalted peanuts
cilantro leaves

A smart, speedy lunch you can prep in advance. Full of vegetables, flavor, and gut-friendly goodness, just add hot water, shake, and you've got soup in minutes.

Before you start: you will need 2 x 1-quart (1-liter) glass canning jars—make sure they are heatproof.

Prep ingredients. Drain and press the tofu with paper towels to remove any excess moisture. Cut the tofu into small bite-sized chunks. Slice the carrot into long ribbons using a vegetable peeler or mandoline. Trim the bok choy and roughly chop. Thinly slice the corn, shiitake mushrooms, and green onions. Halve the sugar snap peas. Peel and grate the ginger, and juice the lime.

Get layering. Mix together the miso, soy sauce, sesame oil, rice wine vinegar, maple syrup, grated ginger, and lime juice then divide between the two jars. Layer the noodles, kimchi, tofu, and the prepared carrot, bok choy, baby corn, mushrooms, and sugar snap peas in the jars. Top with the green onions. Cover each jar with a lid and store in the fridge for up to 3 days.

To cook. Ten minutes prior to serving, boil the water and divide evenly into each jar (let cool for a couple of minutes so it's not superhot), ensuring that the contents are completely covered. Cover with the lids and leave for 2 minutes to allow the noodles to heat through and the vegetables to soften slightly. Carefully, open the lids to release any pressure and heat. Put the lids on again and shake well to mix up the noodle and vegetables broth.

Assemble and serve. Carefully reopen each jar slowly and transfer the contents to a bowl to serve or eat straight from the jar. Garnish with crispy onions, chopped peanuts, and cilantro, if you like.

1/2 LITRE
400 ml
350 ml
300 ml
1/4 LITRE
200 ml
150 ml

LOADED BUFFALO CHICKPEA BAGELS

PER PORTION:

- **8 PLANT POINTS**
- **27g PROTEIN**
- **679 kcal**

Serves 4

For the buffalo chickpeas

1 x 25oz (700g) can chickpeas
2 tsp olive oil
2 tsp sweet smoked paprika
⅓ cup (100ml) hot sauce, plus extra to serve
2 tsp maple (or agave) syrup
sea salt and freshly ground black pepper
4 seedy bagels, preferably whole wheat, to serve

For the cashew cream

1⅓ cup (150g) raw cashews
⅔ cup (140ml) plant-based milk, plus extra if needed
1oz (25g) nutritional yeast
1 tsp garlic powder
1 tsp onion powder
½ tsp sweet smoked paprika
½ tsp sea salt

For the green onion cream

3 green onions
1 tomato
¼oz (10g) dill fronds, plus extra to serve
2 tbsp capers
1 lemon

Bagels are a beautiful thing—especially if you're carb-loading before a big race (just ask Ian, who smashed loads of these before running his first ultra marathon in July '25). Spicy buffalo chickpeas, silky cashew cream, and a tangy green onion topping come together for the ultimate pre-run power-up.

Before you start: you will need a high-speed blender. Line a large baking sheet with parchment paper (if using the oven). Preheat the air fryer to 350°F (180°C) or oven to 400°F (200°C).

Prep chickpeas. Drain and rinse the chickpeas, then pat dry with paper towels. Pour the chickpeas into a mixing bowl, drizzle over the olive oil, and season with paprika, salt, and pepper, then toss to coat them in the seasoned oil. Transfer to the preheated air fryer and cook for 15 minutes, until slightly golden. (Alternatively, place on a lined baking sheet and roast in the oven for 15–20 minutes.)

Make cashew cream. Meanwhile, place the cashews in a heatproof bowl and pour over enough just-boiled water to cover. Let cashews soak for 10 minutes to soften, then drain and place in a blender. Add the rest of the cashew cream ingredients and blend until smooth, adding a dash more plant-based milk, if needed, to make a smooth cream—it should be thick enough to coat the chickpeas. Split the cream between 2 large bowls.

Make buffalo chickpeas. Pour the hot sauce and maple syrup into one of the bowls of cashew cream. Taste and adjust the seasoning, adding more salt and pepper, if needed. Stir in the roasted chickpeas until coated in the cream.

Make green onion cream. Finely slice the green onions and finely dice the tomato. Roughly chop the dill and add to the second bowl of cashew cream with the green onions and tomato. Add the capers and squeeze in the juice of the lemon to taste, and stir to combine. Taste and season with salt and pepper, if needed.

Assemble and serve. Halve and toast the bagels. Spread the green onion cream over the base of each bagel. Spoon over the buffalo chickpeas and finish with extra hot sauce and dill. Top each one with the other half of the bagel.

SMASHED POTATO & CUCUMBER SALAD (WITH SESAME MAYO DRESSING)

PER PORTION:

- **6.75 PLANT POINTS**
- **8.5g PROTEIN**
- **552 kcal**

Serves about 4

2¼lb (1kg) baby new potatoes
2 tbsp olive oil
1 cucumber
4 green onions
½oz (15g) cilantro
2 tbsp crispy chili oil
1 tbsp black sesame seeds

For the sesame mayo dressing
1 lime
2 tbsp tahini
1 tbsp toasted sesame oil
1 tbsp white miso
3½oz (100g) plant-based mayo
sea salt and freshly ground black pepper

Crispy smashed potatoes meet crunchy cucumber in this bold, brilliant salad. Coated in a rich sesame mayo, the potatoes are finished with chili oil and herbs—and yep, it banged on our socials.

Before you start: you will need a large saucepan. Line a large baking sheet with parchment paper (if using the oven). Preheat the air fryer to 400°F (200°C) or oven to 425°F (220°C).

Prep potatoes. Place the potatoes in a large saucepan of salted cold water. Bring to a boil and cook for around 10 minutes, until tender but still holding together. Drain the potatoes and let steam-dry in the pan for a few minutes.

Air-fry potatoes. Put the potatoes onto a cutting board and carefully crush (without completely breaking them apart) with the bottom of a glass or the back of a fork. Drizzle with the olive oil. Put in the preheated air fryer and cook for 15–20 minutes, until golden and crisp. (Alternatively, roast in the preheated oven on a lined baking sheet for 25 minutes, turning halfway.)

Make sesame mayo dressing. Meanwhile, in a small bowl, zest and juice the lime. Add the tahini, sesame oil, miso, plant-based mayo, and 3 tablespoons water, and whisk to combine. Taste and season with salt and pepper. Set aside.

Prep salad. Slice the cucumber in half lengthwise. Scoop out the seedy center with a spoon and slice the cucumber into half-moons. Finely chop the green onions. Pick the cilantro leaves.

Assemble and serve. Place the potatoes in a large bowl with the cucumber, green onions, and cilantro leaves. Add the sesame mayo dressing and toss together to coat. Transfer to a serving platter, drizzle over the crispy chili oil, and sprinkle with black sesame seeds before serving.

HAZELNUT PESTO COUSCOUS SALAD

PER PORTION:

- 9.25 PLANT POINTS
- 70g PROTEIN
- 905 kcal

Serves 4

9oz (250g) couscous, preferably whole grain
1 cup (250ml) water
2 tsp vegetable bouillon powder
9oz (250g) frozen shelled edamame
5 green onions
5–6 sun-dried tomatoes in oil, drained
20oz (570g) cooked chickpeas
3½oz (100g) Kalamata olives, preferably pitted

For the pesto (or use store-bought basil pesto)
½ cup(75g) blanched hazelnuts
1 lemon
1 small garlic clove
½ cup(125ml) extra-virgin olive oil
1½ cups(50g) basil leaves
1¾oz(50g) nutritional yeast
sea salt and freshly ground black pepper

This easy couscous salad is perfect for lunches, barbecues, or batch prep. It comes with plant protein and a zingy, herby pesto, and is packed with freshness, flavor, and crunch.

Before you start: you will need a small skillet and a food processor (or high-speed blender or pestle and mortar).

Make pesto. Toast the hazelnuts in a small skillet over medium heat, tossing regularly, for 3–4 minutes, until golden. Pour the nuts into a bowl and let cool. Halve the lemon, then juice one half and cut the other half into wedges. Peel the garlic. Add three-quarters of the hazelnuts with the juice of the lemon, the garlic, olive oil, basil, and nutritional yeast to a food processor and pulse to a chunky pesto. Season with salt, pepper, and more nutritional yeast, if you like.

Cook couscous. Add the couscous to a heatproof bowl along with 5 tablespoons of the pesto and mix well to combine. Pour the 1 cup (250ml) of just-boiled water over the couscous and stir in the bouillon powder, cover with a plate, and leave for 5 minutes, until the grains are tender and the water has been absorbed. Fluff up the couscous with a fork.

Cook edamame. Meanwhile, place the edamame in a heatproof bowl, pour over just-boiled water from a kettle to cover and leave for a few minutes to defrost. Drain and rinse under cold running water.

Finish couscous. Finely slice the green onions and finely chop the sun-dried tomatoes. Drain and rinse the chickpeas. Add the green onions, sun-dried tomatoes, edamame, chickpeas and olives to the couscous, season with salt and pepper to taste, and stir to combine.

Assemble and serve. Transfer the couscous salad to a serving bowl. Roughly chop the remaining hazelnuts and sprinkle them over, then add dollops of the remaining pesto, if you like. Serve with the lemon wedges for squeezing over.

Store. If not serving right away, store in the fridge in one large or individual containers for up to 2 days.

SMOKY ROASTED ROMESCO SOUP

PER PORTION:

- 7.25 PLANT POINTS
- 14g PROTEIN
- 490 kcal

Serves 4

4 large red peppers
1 large red onion
3 medium sweet potatoes
4 garlic cloves
3 tbsp olive oil
¾ cup (100g) blanched almonds
1 x 14.5oz (411g) can chopped tomatoes
2 tbsp sweet smoked paprika, plus extra to serve
large pinch of chili flakes (for a bit of heat, optional)
6¼ cups (1.5 liters) hot vegetable stock
1 tbsp sherry (or red wine) vinegar
pinch of sugar (optional)
extra-virgin olive oil, for drizzling
sea salt and freshly ground black pepper

Deeply smoky, rich, and full of flavor, this vibrant soup blends roasted peppers, sweet potatoes, and almonds for a warming bowl that tastes even better the next day.

Before you start: you will need a large saucepan and an immersion blender (or high-speed blender). Line 2 large baking sheets with parchment paper. Preheat the oven to 425°F (220°C).

Prep vegetables. Slice the peppers into strips, discarding the seedy cores. Peel the onion and cut into thin wedges. Peel the sweet potatoes and cut into small, bite-sized chunks.

Roast vegetables. Place the peppers, onion, and unpeeled garlic on one of the lined baking sheets. Place the sweet potatoes on a separate lined baking sheet. Drizzle each one with half of the olive oil and season with salt and pepper. Roast in the preheated oven for about 20 minutes, until the vegetables are almost cooked. Add the almonds to the tray containing the sweet potatoes and roast for a further 5 minutes. All the vegetables and the garlic should be soft, and starting to blacken in places, and the nuts turning golden.

Make soup. Transfer the roasted peppers, onion, sweet potatoes, and toasted almonds (saving a few to garnish) to a large saucepan. Squeeze in the roasted garlic, discarding the skins. Add the canned tomatoes, along with the smoked paprika and chili flakes, if using, then pour in the hot vegetable stock. Bring the soup up to a simmer and cook for about 5 minutes to allow the flavors to develop, then add the vinegar.

Blend soup. Using an immersion blender, blend the soup until smooth (or transfer the soup to a blender and blend in batches). Return the soup to low heat and taste, adding salt, pepper, and more vinegar or a pinch of sugar, if needed.

Assemble and serve. Ladle the soup into bowls and drizzle with extra-virgin olive oil, then sprinkle over the reserved toasted almonds and an extra pinch of smoked paprika.

Store. If not serving right away, store in an airtight container in the fridge for up to 3 days or freeze for up to 3 months.

BRIGHT GREEN FALAFEL

PER FALAFEL:
- 5.5 PLANT POINTS
- 2.5g PROTEIN
- 54 kcal

Makes 22–24

2 × 15oz (439g) cans chickpeas
¾ cup (30g) cilantro
¾ cup (30g) parsley
1 small onion (or 3 green onions)
3 garlic cloves
1⅔ cup(50g) spinach leaves
2 tsp ground cumin
1 tsp ground cilantro
5 tbsp chickpea flour (or all-purpose flour)
1 tbsp lemon juice
1 tbsp olive oil, plus extra for cooking the falafel
½ tsp sea salt
pinch of freshly ground black pepper

We couldn't release a book called *More Plants* without a falafel recipe. These bright green beauties are herby, crispy on the outside, soft in the middle, and absolutely packed with flavor. They're perfect served in a wrap with all the classic trimmings or in a bowl with grains, fresh vegetables, tahini, and hummus.

Before you start: you will need a food processor. Line a large baking sheet with parchment paper (if using the oven). Preheat the air fryer to 400°F (200°C) or oven to 425°F (220°C).

Prep ingredients. Drain the chickpeas. Pick the parsley and cilantro leaves, discarding the stalks. Peel and roughly chop the onion and garlic.

Make falafel mix. Add the chickpeas, onion, garlic, cilantro, parsley, and spinach to a food processor and pulse until finely chopped but not completely smooth. Add the ground spices, chickpea flour, lemon juice, and olive oil. Pulse until the mixture comes together in a firm, thick, coarse paste. If it's too loose, add a little more flour.

Cook falafel. Form the mixture into 22–24 falafel-shaped balls (slightly smaller than a golf ball). Drizzle or spray with olive oil and cook in the preheated air fryer for 13–15 minutes, until golden brown. (Alternatively, bake in the preheated oven on a lined baking sheet for 16–18 minutes.)

Serve. Serve warm or at room temperature with all your favorite extras.

Store. If not serving right away, store in an airtight container in the fridge for up to 3 days or freeze for up to 3 months.

KOREAN KIMCHI GRAIN BOWL (WITH MISO TAHINI DRIZZLE)

PER PORTION:

- 10.25 PLANT POINTS
- 32g PROTEIN
- 857 kcal

Serves 2

For the grains
1¾oz (50g) quinoa
1¾oz (50g) bulgur wheat
1¾oz (50g) millet
2 cups (500ml) vegetable stock
1 tbsp gochujang paste

For the miso-tahini drizzle
2 tbsp toasted sesame oil
1 tbsp tamari
1 tbsp rice wine vinegar
1 tbsp white miso
2 tbsp tahini
2 tsp maple (or agave) syrup
1 lime

For the rest
7oz (200g) frozen shelled edamame beans
handful of radishes
1 avocado
3–4 tbsp Protein Packed seed blend (see p208)
2 tsp gochugaru
4¼oz (120g) kimchi

A vibrant, flavor-packed bowl with plenty of texture and zing. Nutty grains, crunchy vegetables, creamy avocado, gut-friendly kimchi, and a punchy miso-tahini drizzle come together for a balanced, satisfying lunch or dinner.

Before you start: you will need a large saucepan with lid.

Cook grains. Rinse the grains in a sieve under cold running water until the water runs clear, then drain. Add the grains to a large saucepan, pour over the vegetable stock to cover, and add the gochujang. Stir until combined and bring up to a boil over high heat. Once boiling, reduce the heat to low, cover with the lid, and cook for 15 minutes, until the stock is absorbed and the grains are tender. Remove the pan from the heat and set aside in the covered pan until ready to serve.

Make miso-tahini drizzle. Meanwhile, whisk together the drizzle ingredients until combined. Gradually add 4 tablespoons water until the mixture has the consistency of cream (the tahini may thicken initially but will loosen with the addition of more water).

Prep the rest. Cook the edamame in boiling salted water for 3–4 minutes, then drain and set aside to cool. Very thinly slice the radishes. Quarter the avocado, removing the stone and skin. Mix the seed blend on a small plate with the gochugaru. Place the avocado, cut-side down, into the seed mixture, applying a little pressure so that the seeds adhere.

Assemble and serve. Divide the grains, kimchi, edamame, radishes, and seeded avocado between serving bowls. Generously drizzle over the miso-tahini dressing and top with any remaining seed mix.

ZERO WASTE SUPER-GREEN BEANS

PER PORTION:
- **9 PLANT POINTS**
- **40g PROTEIN**
- **697 kcal**

Serves 2

1 large head of broccoli
7oz (200g) Tuscan kale leaves
½ unwaxed lemon
1⅔ cup(50g) baby spinach leaves
1oz (25g) nutritional yeast
1 vegetable stock pot
2 x 15.5oz (439g) cans lima beans
sea salt and freshly ground black pepper

For the crunchy topper
2 tbsp olive oil
3 tbsp Protein Packed seed blend (see p208)
OR
1 small handful of chopped walnuts
1 tbsp sunflower seeds
1 tbsp mixed seeds
1 tsp nutritional yeast

To serve
extra-virgin olive oil
slices of sourdough, preferably whole wheat

A vibrant, feel-good dish that makes the most of every bit of broccoli. Creamy, lemony, high in fiber, and packed with green vegetables, the beans are delicious sprinkled with crunchy seeds and served with slices of sourdough toast and a drizzle of olive oil.

Before you start: you will need a large frying (or griddle) pan, a large saucepan, and a high-speed blender.

Prep ingredients. Dice the broccoli stalk into ½ in(1cm) cubes and cut the head into small florets, then divide the stalk/florets into two portions. Strip the kale leaves off the stalks, then finely chop the stalks and roughly chop the leaves. Zest and juice the lemon.

Make crunchy topper. Add the olive oil to a large skillet over medium–high heat. Add one half of the broccoli stalk/florets and season with salt and pepper. Leave the pan alone for 2–3 minutes, until the broccoli is charred in places, then give everything a stir and repeat this cooking process twice more, stirring each time, until the broccoli is charred all over. Add the seed blend (or the chopped walnuts and seeds) and toast for a minute or two. Remove from the heat and sprinkle with nutritional yeast, if using the walnut seed mix, and toss lightly to combine. Pour into a bowl and set aside.

Make green sauce. Bring a large saucepan of lightly salted water to a boil. Add the remaining broccoli stalk/florets and kale stalks and cook for 6–7 minutes, until soft and fork-tender. Add the spinach and kale leaves and cook for another minute until wilted. Drain well, reserving a cupful of the cooking water. Add the greens to a blender along with the nutritional yeast, stock pot, and lemon zest and juice, then blend until smooth, adding a little of the reserved cooking water, if needed. Taste and season with salt and pepper. Pour the sauce back into the pan.

Prep lima beans. Drain the beans and fold them into the green sauce in the pan. Warm over low heat until heated through (keeping the heat low will help keep the greens bright).

Assemble and serve. Spoon the super-green beans into a serving dish, then sprinkle over the crunchy broccoli topper. Drizzle over a little olive oil to finish and serve warm with slices of sourdough, preferably toasted.

SPICY SOBA SATAY SALAD (WITH SMOKY TEMPEH CROUTONS)

PER PORTION:
- **7.75 PLANT POINTS**
- **50g PROTEIN**
- **1,030 kcal**

Serves 2

For the salad
5½oz (150g) broccolini
1 red hot, sweet pepper
¼ onion
large handful of cilantro leaves
7oz (200g) dried soba noodles, preferably whole wheat

For the peanut sauce
1 lime
3 tbsp(50g) peanut butter (smooth or crunchy)
3 tbsp (40ml) light soy sauce (or tamari)
1 tbsp toasted sesame oil
2 tbsp Spicy nooch blend (see p212), or nutritional yeast
1 tbsp maple (or agave) syrup
2 tbsp sriracha
4 tbsp water

For the smoky tempeh croutons
7oz (200g) tempeh
2 tbsp toasted sesame oil
pinch of sea salt
2 tbsp light soy sauce (or tamari)
2 tsp maple (or agave) syrup
2 tsp liquid smoke (optional)

To serve
roasted unsalted peanuts
slices of red chile

If you're new to tempeh, start here. You won't be disappointed. Big flavors, perfect textures, and a great dish for warm weather. This one's a keeper.

Before you start: you will need a large saucepan, a high-speed blender, and a small skillet.

Prep salad. Slice the broccolini into 2in (5cm) long pieces, leaving the florets whole. Very thinly slice the pepper, discarding the seeds, and onion. Pick the cilantro leaves.

Cook broccolini and noodles. Bring a large saucepan of water to a boil. Cook the broccolini for 2–3 minutes, until tender but still with some bite. Remove with a slotted spoon and set aside in a large serving bowl. In the same boiling water, cook the soba noodles according to the package instructions. Drain and rinse well under cold running water. Drain again, then add to the bowl with the broccolini.

Make peanut sauce. Squeeze the juice of 1 lime into a blender. Add the rest of the sauce ingredients, then blend until super-smooth. Alternatively, simply whisk together all the ingredients until well combined.

Combine. Add two-thirds of the peanut sauce to the broccolini and noodles and set aside for at least 10 minutes to allow the noodles and broccolini to soak up all the saucy flavors.

Make and cook tempeh croutons. Meanwhile, crumble the tempeh into small pieces. Heat the sesame oil in a small skillet over medium–high heat. Add the tempeh and a pinch of salt and cook, stirring regularly, for 7–8 minutes, until golden brown and crispy. Reduce the heat to low, add the soy sauce, maple syrup, and liquid smoke, if using, and cook, stirring for another minute or two until caramelized. Set aside to cool.

Assemble and serve. Add the tempeh and veggies and most of the cilantro leaves to the noodles and broccolini. Add the remaining peanut sauce and toss to combine. To serve, add chopped peanuts, the remaining cilantro, and sliced red chile.

SMOKED TOFU SUMMER ROLLS

PER ROLL:
- **7.75 PLANT POINTS**
- **8.5g PROTEIN**
- **174 kcal**

Makes about 16

For the rolls
7oz (200g) dried vermicelli rice noodles, preferably whole wheat
⅔ cup (25g) mint
⅔ cup (25g) cilantro
2 carrots
1 Baby Gem lettuce
2 ripe, small stone fruit, such as peaches or nectarines (or 1 large stone fruit, such as mango)
20oz (560g) extra-firm smoked tofu
2 tbsp neutral oil of your choice, plus extra for greasing plate/tray
pinch of sea salt
1 tbsp hoisin sauce
1 tbsp light soy sauce (or tamari)
16 rice paper spring roll wrappers

For the nuoc cham
1 garlic clove
1 red chile
3 tbsp light soy sauce (or vegan fish sauce)
2 tbsp sugar
1 lime
4 tbsp water

For the peanut sauce
2 limes
5 tbsp smooth peanut butter
1 tbsp light soy sauce (or tamari)

Fresh and fun to make, these rice-paper rolls are packed with noodles, herbs, crisp vegetables, and sticky smoked tofu. They're perfect for dipping and sharing for a light, summery lunch.

Before you start: you will need a large saucepan and a large skillet.

Prep filling for rolls. Cook the noodles following the package instructions. Drain and rinse under cold running water, then set aside. Pick the mint and cilantro leaves. Slice the carrots into matchsticks or julienne strips. Finely shred the lettuce. Remove the stone from the fruit and slice into thin strips or wedges. Arrange everything on plates/bowls, ready to assemble your summer rolls.

Cook tofu. Drain the tofu and pat dry with paper towels to remove any excess moisture. Slice the tofu into ½ in (1 cm) strips. Heat the oil in a large skillet over medium–high heat. Add the tofu and a pinch of salt and fry for 7–8 minutes, turning until golden all over. Add the hoisin and soy sauce and cook for a further minute, turning, until the tofu is golden and sticky.

Make nuoc cham. Peel and grate the garlic. Finely chop the chile. Put the garlic and chile in a small bowl with the soy sauce and sugar. Squeeze in the juice of 1 lime and add the water, then stir until the sugar dissolves.

Make peanut sauce. Juice the 2 limes in a bowl, then stir in the peanut butter and soy sauce. Add a little water, if needed, to achieve a dipping consistency.

Assemble and serve. Briefly dip a rice-paper wrapper in warm water until soft and pliable, remove from the water and lay on a dish towel. Place a small bundle of noodles, a few strips of smoked tofu, some lettuce, carrot, stone fruit, and herb leaves down the middle of the wrapper. Fold up the bottom and one side of the wrapper over the filling, then continue to roll tightly to enclose the filling and make a cylinder shape. Continue to make about 16 rolls in total with the rest of the wrappers and filling ingredients, placing them on a lightly oiled plate or tray when ready. Serve the summer rolls alongside the bowls of peanut sauce and/or nuoc cham for dipping.

SWEET CHILI TOFU LETTUCE CUPS

PER PORTION:
- **8.25 PLANT POINTS**
- **41g PROTEIN**
- **650 kcal**

Serves 2

16oz (450g) extra-firm tofu
2 Baby Gem lettuces
1 onion
1 red pepper
3 garlic cloves
1 thumb-sized piece of fresh ginger
3 tbsp light soy sauce
2 tbsp cornstarch
3 tbsp neutral oil of your choice
4 tbsp sweet chili sauce, plus extra to serve

For quick pickled carrot
1 carrot
1 lime
pinch of sugar
pinch of sea salt, plus extra to season

To serve
toasted sesame seeds
cilantro leaves (optional)

Packed with flavor, these fresh, crunchy lettuce cups are loaded with crispy tofu, a sticky-sweet sauce, and zingy pickles. Fun to eat, quick to make, and endlessly satisfying.

Before you start: you will need a large skillet.

Pickle carrot. First make the quick pickled carrot. Finely slice the carrot into julienne strips. Halve the lime and slice one half into wedges and set aside for later. Add the carrot to a small bowl, squeeze in the juice of the remaining ½ lime, then sprinkle with the sugar and salt and stir well to combine. Set aside to pickle.

Prep ingredients. Drain the tofu, pressing it with paper towels to remove any excess moisture, then tear into bite-sized chunks. Trim the lettuces, separate the leaves and arrange them on a plate. Peel and finely slice the onion and red pepper, discarding the seedy core. Peel and grate the garlic and ginger.

Cook tofu. Mix 2 tablespoons of the soy sauce with the cornstarch in a bowl. Add the tofu and toss to lightly coat each piece. Heat 2 tablespoons of the oil in a large skillet over medium–high heat and fry for 7–8 minutes, until golden and crisp all over. Remove from the pan with a slotted spoon and set aside briefly.

Finish tofu. Add the remaining oil to the same skillet over medium–high heat. Add the onion and pepper and stir-fry for 2–3 minutes, until tender but still with a little bite. Add the garlic and ginger and cook for 30–60 seconds, until fragrant, making sure the garlic doesn't burn. Return the tofu to the pan, drizzle in the sweet chili sauce and the remaining soy sauce. Toss well and cook for another minute until everything is coated and lightly caramelized. Taste and season with salt, if needed.

Assemble and serve. Bring the sweet chili tofu and lettuce cups to the table for everyone to assemble themselves. Serve with the pickled carrot, extra sweet chili sauce, a sprinkling of sesame seeds, cilantro leaves, if using, and the lime wedges for squeezing more juice over.

ml
250
200
150
100
50

CRISPY TEMPEH, RICE & CUCUMBER SALAD

PER PORTION:
- 4.75 PLANT POINTS
- 36g PROTEIN
- 966 kcal

Serves 2

7oz (200g) tempeh
2 tbsp neutral oil of your choice
9oz (250g) cooked cold jasmine rice, preferably brown
1 tbsp light soy sauce
1 tbsp maple (or agave) syrup
1 tbsp toasted sesame oil
1 cucumber
1 red chile
1 handful each of mint and cilantro, plus extra to garnish
⅓ cup (50g) unsalted roasted peanuts, plus extra to garnish

For the dressing
2 limes
4 tbsp plant-based mayo
1 tbsp light soy sauce
1 tbsp maple (or agave) syrup
2 tsp crispy chili oil
sea salt

Fresh, crisp and full of flavor, this salad combines crispy tempeh, rice, fresh herbs, and a punchy chili-lime dressing for a quick meal that feels anything but basic.

Before you start: you will need a large skillet (or wok).

Crispy tempeh and rice. Coarsely grate the tempeh using a cheese grater. Heat the oil over medium-high heat in a large skillet, add the tempeh and rice, and stir-fry for about 10 minutes, until golden and crisp. Stir in the soy sauce, maple syrup, and sesame oil, then cook for a minute or so until the tempeh and rice are coated. Pour into a bowl and let cool.

Prep salad ingredients. Meanwhile, finely slice the cucumber and chile into rounds. Finely chop the herbs and roughly chop the peanuts.

Make dressing. Squeeze the juice of 1 lime into a bowl and cut the other into wedges, setting it aside for later. Add the rest of the dressing ingredients to the bowl and whisk to combine. Season with salt and extra lime juice, if needed.

Assemble and serve. Combine the cooled tempeh and rice with the rest of the salad ingredients in a large bowl. Pour over the dressing and toss well until combined. Garnish with extra peanuts and herbs, then serve with the lime wedges by the side for squeezing more juice over.

PURPLE PRINCESS SALAD

PER PORTION:
- 8.25 PLANT POINTS
- 13g PROTEIN
- 328 kcal

Serves 4

9oz (250g) frozen shelled edamame
⅓ red cabbage
1 tbsp extra-virgin olive oil
sea salt
1 cucumber
3 cooked beets (not in vinegar)
3 large oranges

For the dressing
2 lemons
2 tbsp tahini
2 tbsp extra-virgin olive oil
⅓ cup (100ml) water
sea salt and freshly ground black pepper

To serve
nutritional yeast
Protein Packed seed blend (see p208)

You've heard of the green goddess; now meet the purple princess. Vibrant, high in protein, and full of texture, this salad is as nourishing as it is beautiful. If preferred, use raw beets, rather than cooked, and roast in the oven or air fry with a splash of olive oil until tender.

Before you start: you will need a high-speed blender.

Prep vegetables. Place the edamame in a heatproof bowl, pour over just-boiled water to cover and leave for a few minutes to defrost, then drain. Shred the cabbage and add to a bowl with the olive oil and a little salt. Massage the oil into the cabbage with your hands until softened. Finely slice the cucumber into rounds. Cut the beets into wedges.

Prep fruit. Peel the oranges with a small, sharp knife. Next, hold one of the oranges over a bowl and, with the knife, carefully cut along the white membrane of each segment to remove the orange slice. Place the orange segments in a bowl, saving any juices. Repeat with the remaining 2 oranges.

Make dressing. Juice both lemons and add to a blender with half of the beets, the tahini, extra-virgin olive oil, and water. Season with salt and pepper. Blend until smooth, adding a little extra water, if needed, to make a thick, creamy dressing. Set aside, ideally in a squeezy bottle.

Assemble and serve. Add the edamame, cucumber, and orange (and any juices) to the bowl with the cabbage and toss to combine. Transfer the salad to a serving dish, add the remaining beets, drizzle or dollop over the beet dressing, then finish with a sprinkling of nutritional yeast and the seed blend to serve.

Store. If not serving right away, store in the fridge in one large or individual containers for up to 2 days. Stir well before serving to redistribute the dressing.

SUNNY DITALINI PASTA SALAD (WITH ORANGE SHALLOT DRESSING)

PER PORTION:

- 5.75 PLANT POINTS
- 20g PROTEIN
- 700 kcal

Serves 4

For the crispy shallots
3 shallots
⅓ cup (100ml) extra-virgin olive oil
good pinch of sea salt

For the salad
12oz (350g) ditalini
2 fennel bulbs
3 blood oranges (regular oranges are also fine)
1 x 15.5oz (439g) can chickpeas
large handful of parsley leaves
large handful of dill fronds
3 tbsp Gut Health seed blend (see p209)

For the dressing
2 blood oranges (or regular ones)
1 tbsp Dijon mustard
2 tsp red wine vinegar
1 tsp sea salt
1 tsp cracked black pepper

This vibrant, zesty, flavor-packed salad is perfect for warmer days, and definitely one to take to a barbecue. P.S. Ditalini might just become your new favorite pasta shape.

Before you start: you will need a small saucepan and a large saucepan.

Prep and cook shallots. Peel and cut the shallots in half lengthwise, then thinly slice. Add the olive oil and shallots to a small saucepan and season with a good pinch of salt. Set the pan over medium heat until the oil starts to sizzle. Continue to cook for 5–10 minutes (depending on the thickness of your shallots), until golden brown and crispy. Strain through a metal sieve, saving the oil in a bowl to use for the dressing. Set the crispy shallots aside for garnishing.

Cook pasta. Meanwhile, bring a large saucepan of salted water to the boil, add the ditalini and cook according to the package instructions. Drain and rinse well under cold running water to cool and prevent it from sticking together. Put the pasta in a large bowl and set aside.

Prep salad ingredients. Slice the fennel very thinly with a knife or mandoline. Peel the oranges with a small knife or use your fingers. Once the skin/pith is removed, slice the oranges into thin rounds and set aside. Drain and rinse the chickpeas. Roughly chop the parsley and dill, ready for assembling.

Make dressing. Finely grate the zest of 1 orange and squeeze the juice of both oranges into the bowl containing the shallot frying oil. Add the rest of the dressing ingredients and whisk well until combined.

Assemble and serve. Add all the prepared salad ingredients to the bowl of pasta, reserving some of the fennel, orange slices, and herbs for topping. Pour the dressing over and give everything a good mix, then taste and adjust the seasoning, if needed. Top with the reserved fennel, orange slices, and herbs. Sprinkle over the seed blend and the crispy shallots to serve.

MEDITERRANEAN SPELT SALAD

PER PORTION:
- 11.5 PLANT POINTS
- 19g PROTEIN
- 731 kcal

Serves 4

10oz (300g) spelt (or use 2 ready-cooked spelt microwave pouches—about 18oz/500g cooked weight)
4 tbsp pine nuts (or sunflower seeds)
14oz (400g) cherry tomatoes
2 cucumbers
1 small red onion (swap for a few green onions, if preferred)
7oz (200g) artichoke hearts, drained
7oz (200g) pitted green (or black) olives
2 roasted red peppers in oil from a jar (or 2 fresh red peppers)
2 small handfuls of basil leaves
2 small handfuls of parsley
2 tbsp capers
½oz (15g) nutritional yeast

For the dressing
4 tbsp extra-virgin olive oil
2 lemons
1 tbsp dried oregano
sea salt and freshly ground black pepper

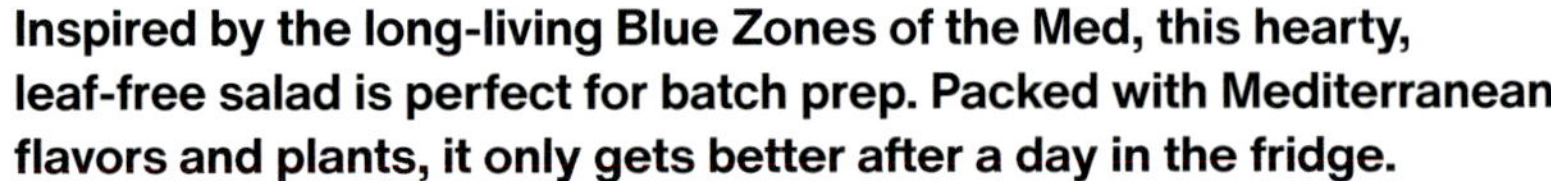

Inspired by the long-living Blue Zones of the Med, this hearty, leaf-free salad is perfect for batch prep. Packed with Mediterranean flavors and plants, it only gets better after a day in the fridge.

Before you start: you will need a medium saucepan and a small skillet.

Cook spelt. If using uncooked spelt, cook it in a medium saucepan of boiling water for around 25 minutes, until the grains are tender with a little bite. Drain and rinse under cold running water. Set aside to cool further.

Toast nuts. Meanwhile, heat a small skillet over medium heat until hot. Add the pine nuts and toast, tossing regularly, for 3–4 minutes, until light golden. Pour into a bowl and let cool.

Prep salad. Halve the tomatoes. Halve each cucumber lengthwise, scoop out the seeds and discard, then slice into half-moons. Thinly slice the onion and drain the artichokes. Roughly chop most of the artichokes and olives, keeping some whole to garnish. Dice the roasted peppers or fresh peppers, discarding the seedy cores. Roughly tear the herbs.

Make dressing. Whisk the extra-virgin olive oil with the juice of both lemons and the oregano. Season with salt and pepper to taste.

Assemble and serve. In a large bowl, combine the spelt, tomatoes, cucumbers, onion, chopped artichokes and olives, peppers, capers, and nutritional yeast. Pour the dressing over and toss thoroughly. Spoon the salad into a serving bowl, sprinkle over the reserved whole olives, artichokes, and toasted pine nuts.

Store. If not serving right away, store in the fridge in one large or individual containers for up to 2 days. Stir well before serving to redistribute the dressing.

CHICKPEA "TUNA" PASTA SALAD

PER PORTION:

- **6 PLANT POINTS**
- **24g PROTEIN**
- **816 kcal**

Serves 2

7oz (200g) short pasta, such as penne or fusilli, preferably whole wheat
1 x 14oz (400g) can young green jackfruit in water or brine (not in syrup)
1 x 15.5oz (439g) can chickpeas
2 green onions
1 celery stalk
2 sheets nori
2 tbsp capers in brine

For the dressing
5 tbsp plant-based mayonnaise
1 tsp Dijon mustard
1 tbsp lemon juice
¼ tsp garlic powder (optional)
sea salt and freshly ground black pepper

We've given tuna pasta salad a *More Plants* makeover. With seaside-inspired flavors and a mix of textures, this is ideal for work lunches or light dinners.

Before you start: you will need a large saucepan.

Cook pasta. Bring a large saucepan of salted water to a boil, add the pasta, and cook according to the package instructions. Drain and rinse well under cold running water to cool and prevent it from sticking together. Put the pasta in a large bowl and set aside.

Prep ingredients. While the pasta is cooking, drain and rinse the jackfruit, then roughly chop to form tuna fishlike flakes. Drain and rinse the chickpeas and coarsely mash with a fork. Finely slice the green onions and celery. Slice or cut the nori with scissors into very small pieces. Drain and roughly chop the capers.

Make the dressing. In a small bowl, combine the mayonnaise, mustard, lemon juice, and garlic powder, if using. Season with salt and pepper to taste.

Assemble and serve. In a large bowl, add the jackfruit, chickpeas, most of the green onions, celery, capers, and nori. Add the dressing and mix until well combined. Add the pasta and fold it through until coated in the dressing. Check the seasoning, adding more salt and pepper, if needed. Transfer the salad to a serving dish or divide it among bowls to serve. Garnish with the reserved green onions.

Store. If not serving right away, store in the fridge in one large or individual containers for up to 2 days. Stir well before serving to redistribute the dressing.

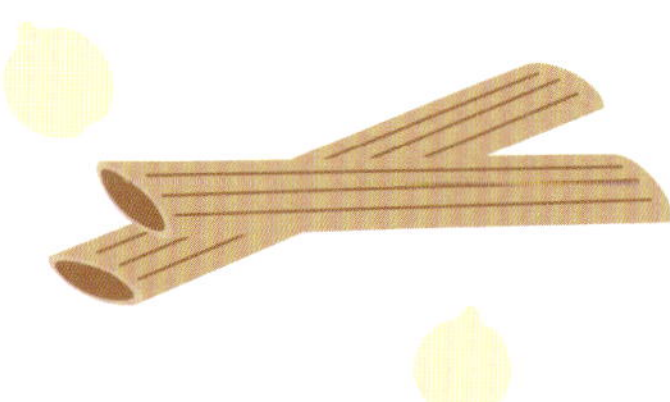

ULTIMATE SUPERFOOD SALAD

PER PORTION:
- **14.25 PLANT POINTS**
- **49g PROTEIN**
- **952 kcal**

Serves 4

3 sweet potatoes
1 small head of broccoli
½ cucumber
25oz (700g) cooked chickpeas
14oz (400g) tempeh
3 tbsp extra-virgin olive oil, divided
good pinch each of sea salt and freshly ground black pepper, plus extra for seasoning
5½oz (150g) quinoa
1¼ cups (300ml) vegetable stock
5½oz (150g) blueberries
7oz (200g) pomegranate seeds

For the dressing
2½ cups(80g) spinach leaves
2 lemons
⅔ cup (25g) basil leaves
⅓ bunch of mint leaves
1 tsp spirulina
1oz (30g) nutritional yeast
1 tbsp Dijon mustard
1 tbsp maple (or agave) syrup
3 tbsp extra-virgin olive oil

For the salad toppers
3½oz (100g) sauerkraut
4 tbsp Brain Power seed blend (see p209)

We don't know what Superman has for lunch, but it's highly likely it's something like this. It checks all the boxes for color, flavor, and nutrition. (Might be worth popping a sticky note on this page!)

Before you start: you will need a small saucepan and a high-speed blender. Line a large roasting pan with parchment paper. Preheat the oven to 425°F (220°C).

Prep salad. Peel and chop the sweet potatoes into 1in (2.5cm) chunks. Chop the broccoli stalk into ¾in(2cm) chunks and cut the head into small florets. Halve cucumber lengthwise, scoop out the seeds using a teaspoon, then slice into half-moons. Drain and rinse the chickpeas. Tear or chop the tempeh into bite-sized chunks.

Roast veggies/tempeh. Add 2 tablespoons of the olive oil to a large bowl and a good pinch of salt and pepper. Add the sweet potatoes, broccoli stalk, and tempeh,and toss well to coat. Pour into the lined roasting pan and cook in the preheated oven for 15 minutes. Using the same bowl, pour in another 1 tablespoon of the olive oil. Add the broccoli florets and toss to coat. After 15 minutes, add the broccoli florets to the roasting pan and cook for a further 15 minutes, until the vegetables and tempeh are golden and tender. Set aside.

Cook quinoa. Meanwhile, rinse the quinoa in a sieve until the water runs clear, then drain. Add the quinoa and stock to a small pan over medium heat. Bring the stock to a gentle simmer, reduce the heat to low, cover, and simmer for 12–15 minutes. Turn off the heat and let the quinoa sit for a further 10 minutes, until tender.

Make dressing. Add the spinach leaves to a heatproof bowl, pour ove just-boiled water, cover, and leave for 60 seconds to wilt. Drain the spinach, then refresh under cold running water. Drain the spinach again, squeezing out as much water as possible. Put the spinach into a blender and squeeze in the juice of both lemons. Add the rest of the dressing ingredients and blend until very smooth. Taste and season with salt and pepper.

Assemble and serve. When the cooked vegetables have cooled, put them in a bowl with the chickpeas, blueberries, and pomegranate seeds, then toss until combined. Transfer to a serving platter, drizzle the dressing over and top with the sauerkraut and seed blend.

MISO, MAPLE & MUSTARD CHOPPED PASTA SALAD

PER PORTION:

- **11.5 PLANT POINTS**
- **17g PROTEIN**
- **533 kcal**

Serves 4

For the salad
9oz (250g) fusilli, penne, orzo, or giant couscous, preferably whole wheat
20oz (570g) cooked chickpeas
5¼oz (160g) sweet corn
1 red pepper
1 small zucchini
1 carrot
½ cucumber
1 celery stalk
4 radishes
3½oz (100g) cherry tomatoes
1 Baby Gem lettuce

For the dressing
3 tbsp extra-virgin olive oil
3 tbsp white miso
3 tbsp maple (or agave) syrup
1 tbsp white wine vinegar
1 tbsp Dijon mustard
1 tbsp dried mixed herbs (or dried parsley, oregano, chives, or basil all work)
⅓ cup (100ml) water
sea salt and freshly ground black pepper

To serve
All the Super Seeds blend of your choice (see pp208–209)

A crunchy, colorful pasta salad with a tangy-sweet dressing that pulls it all together. It's easy to batch; great cold; and packed with flavor, protein, and fresh vegetables.

Before you start: you will need a large saucepan.

Cook pasta. Bring a large saucepan of salted water to a boil, add the pasta and cook according to the package instructions. Drain and rinse well under cold running water to cool and prevent it from sticking together. Put the pasta in a large bowl and set aside.

Prep salad. Meanwhile, drain and rinse the chickpeas and sweet corn. Chop the red pepper, discarding the seedy core, zucchini, carrot, cucumber, celery, and radishes into roughly ½–¾in (1–2cm) chunks. Halve the cherry tomatoes and shred the lettuce.

Make dressing. In a small bowl, combine the extra-virgin olive oil, miso, maple syrup, vinegar, mustard, dried herbs, and water. Taste and season with salt and pepper, and extra maple syrup, vinegar, or mustard, if needed.

Assemble and serve. Add the prepared vegetables to the bowl containing the pasta. Pour the dressing over and toss well to combine.

Store. If not serving right away, store the dressing separately, then dress the salad when you are ready to eat. Both will keep in lidded containers in the fridge for up to 2 days.

CREAMY PEANUT MISO RAMEN

PER PORTION:
- 8.75 PLANT POINTS
- 39g PROTEIN
- 924 kcal

Serves 4

4 garlic cloves
2 in (5 cm) piece of fresh ginger
6 green onions
2 limes
3 tbsp neutral oil of your choice
1 tbsp crispy chili oil, plus extra to serve
2 tbsp white miso
3 tbsp smooth peanut butter
3 tbsp tahini
2 tbsp maple (or agave) syrup
1 tbsp rice wine vinegar
1 x 13.5oz (400ml) can coconut milk
3¼ cups (800ml) vegetable stock
2 tbsp light soy sauce, plus extra to serve
4 baby bok choy
4 x 3½oz (100g) packets of dried ramen noodles (go for whole wheat, if you can find them)

For the tofu crumbles (or use "Beefy" Bits, see p223)
20oz (560g) smoked firm tofu
1 tbsp soy sauce
1 tsp hot smoked paprika
1 tsp liquid smoke (optional)

To serve
black sesame seeds
cilantro leaves

One of our most popular recipes on our socials, and it's easy to see why—a rich, silky broth over noodles, topped with crispy smoked tofu and baby bok choy. Comforting, nourishing, and seriously slurpable, it's one to share on your Instagram stories.

Before you start: you will need a large stock pot (or wok), a large skillet, and a medium saucepan.

Prep ingredients. Peel and grate the garlic and ginger. Finely slice the green onions, separating the green and white parts. Halve the limes and set aside.

Prep broth. Heat 1 tablespoon of the oil with the crispy chili oil in a pot over medium heat. Add the garlic, ginger, and white part of the green onions and fry for 3–4 minutes, until softened. Stir in the miso, peanut butter, tahini, maple syrup, and rice wine vinegar. Pour in the coconut milk and stock, stir, then reduce the heat slightly and simmer while you prepare the rest of the recipe.

Make tofu crumbles. Drain the tofu, pressing with paper towels to remove any excess moisture, then tear roughly into small ¼ in (5 mm) pieces. Heat the remaining 2 tablespoons of oil in a large skillet over medium-high heat. Add the tofu and fry for 7–8 minutes, until golden and crisp. Add the soy sauce, smoked paprika, and liquid smoke, if using, and stir to coat the tofu. Turn the heat down to its lowest setting to keep the tofu warm.

Cook bok choy and noodles. Meanwhile, halve the bok choy lengthwise. Bring a medium saucepan of water to a boil, then reduce the heat to simmering point. Add the bok choy and cook for 1 minute, until wilted, then remove with a slotted spoon. Return the water to a boil, add the noodles (reserving any flavor packets for another recipe), and cook according to the package instructions, about 3–4 minutes, then drain.

Assemble and serve. Taste the broth and season with extra soy sauce and/or lime juice, to taste. Divide the noodles between serving bowls and ladle the broth over. Top with the tofu crumbles and bok choy, then sprinkle with the sesame seeds and the reserved green part of the green onions. Drizzle with extra crispy chili oil and sprinkle over the cilantro, to serve.

PLAN
POIN
DINNE

RS

COCONUT, BASIL & BROCCOLINI NOODLE BROTH
(WITH SPICY PEANUT RAYU)

PER PORTION:
- 7 PLANT POINTS
- 37g PROTEIN
- 1,310 kcal

Serves 2

4 shallots
4 garlic cloves
2 in (5 cm) piece of fresh ginger
1 x 13.5oz (400g) can coconut milk
2 cups (70g) basil or Thai basil
2 tbsp neutral oil of your choice
3 cups (750ml) vegetable stock
5½oz (150g) broccolini
7oz (200g) dried ramen noodles, preferably whole wheat
sesame seeds, to serve

For the spicy peanut rayu
1 lime
⅔ cup (100g) roasted unsalted peanuts
2 tbsp crispy chili oil
1 tbsp light soy sauce
generous pinch of sugar
sea salt

A fragrant, feel-good noodle soup with a creamy coconut and basil broth, zingy aromatics, and just-charred broccolini, and finished with a punchy, nutty peanut rayu for extra heat and crunch; it's comforting, nourishing, and full of vibrant, slurp-able goodness.

Before you start: you will need a high-speed blender, a large saucepan, a medium skillet (or wok), and a medium saucepan.

Prep ingredients. Peel and finely chop the shallots. Peel and grate the garlic and ginger. Blend the coconut milk with the basil until smooth and set aside.

Make broth. Heat half of the oil in a large saucepan over medium–high heat. Add the shallots and ginger and cook for 6–7 minutes, until golden. Add the garlic and cook for another minute. Remove half of the shallot mixture to a small bowl and set aside. Pour the stock into the pan and bring to a simmer. Turn the heat to low and keep the broth on a gentle simmer, topping up with a splash of water, if needed, while you continue with the rest of the recipe.

Make peanut rayu. Juice half of the lime and cut the other half into wedges. Roughly chop the peanuts. Add the crispy chili oil, soy sauce, and peanuts to the reserved fried shallot mixture. Taste and adjust the seasoning with sugar, salt, and the lime juice. Set aside.

Cook broccolini. Heat the remaining 1 tablespoon of oil in a medium skillet over high heat. Add the broccolini with a pinch of salt and stir-fry for 2–3 minutes, until tender and slightly charred in places. Keep warm.

Cook noodles. Meanwhile, cook the noodles following the instructions on the packet, then drain.

Assemble and serve. Divide the coconut basil mixture between your serving bowls, then pour in the hot broth. Add the cooked noodles and top with the charred broccolini. Drizzle generously with the peanut rayu and sprinkle with sesame seeds. Serve with lime wedges for squeezing over.

SPICY PEANUT LIMA BEANS
(WITH GRILLED BOK CHOY)

PER PORTION:
- 8.5 PLANT POINTS
- 24g PROTEIN
- 526 kcal

Serves 2

1 bunch of green onions
3 garlic cloves
1¼ in (3 cm) piece of fresh ginger
1 tbsp chili oil
1½ tbsp smooth peanut butter
1½ tbsp tahini
1–2 tbsp light soy sauce
2 tsp rice wine vinegar
1 cup (200ml) vegetable stock
2 × 15.5oz (439g) cans lima beans
1 tbsp neutral oil of your choice
2 bok choy
sea salt and freshly ground black pepper
Crispy Tofu (see p224), to serve (optional)

To garnish
slices of chile
sesame seeds
cilantro leaves
crispy chili oil

Creamy, nutty lima beans meet smoky, grilled bok choy for a quick, fuss-free midweek dinner. It's hearty, vibrant, and really pretty. Get it on the 'gram!

Before you start: you will need a large, deep skillet with lid and a griddle pan.

Build sauce. Thinly slice the green onions, separating the green and white parts. Peel and grate the garlic and ginger. Heat the chili oil in a large, deep skillet over medium heat. Add the white part of the green onions (save the green part for later) and the ginger and fry for 3–4 minutes, until softened. Stir in the garlic and cook for another minute. Stir in the peanut butter, tahini, soy sauce, vinegar, and stock until combined.

Braise beans. Pour the drained lima beans into the pan and stir gently until the sauce starts to loosen and coat the beans evenly. Bring to a gentle simmer, then reduce the heat to low, part-cover the pan with a lid, and cook for 10–15 minutes, stirring occasionally, until the beans are heated through and the sauce has reduced and thickened. If the sauce gets too thick, add a splash more stock or water.

Cook bok choy. Meanwhile, heat a griddle pan over medium–high heat until hot. Slice the bok choy in half lengthwise and rub a little oil over. Season with salt and pepper. Grill the bok choy for 3 minutes on each side until charred slightly and tender.

Assemble and serve. Top the sesame-peanut beans with the bok choy. Garnish with slices of chile, sesame seeds, the green part of the green onions, and cilantro leaves. Serve topped with crispy tofu, if using, and a drizzle of crispy chili oil.

MISO MUSTARD LIMA BEANS

PER PORTION:
- **7.25 PLANT POINTS**
- **28g PROTEIN**
- **684 kcal**

Serves 4

3 large leeks
4 garlic cloves
1 unwaxed lemon
3 x 15.5oz (439g) cans lima beans
4 tbsp olive oil
4 tbsp Dijon mustard
2 tbsp white miso
½oz (15g) nutritional yeast
9oz (250g) frozen peas
1¼ cups (300ml) plant-based milk

For the bread crumb topping
7oz (200g) sourdough bread, preferably whole wheat
¼ cup (30g) hazelnuts
¼oz (10g) thyme sprigs
3 tbsp olive oil
¼oz (10g) nutritional yeast
sea salt and freshly ground black pepper

Creamy lima beans simmered with leeks, mustard, and miso, then topped with golden hazelnut crumbs. It's rich, comforting, and full of savory flavor. This is what fall tastes like.

Before you start: you will need a food processor and a large, deep, ovenproof skillet.

Prep bread crumb topping. Tear the bread into chunks and add to a food processor with the hazelnuts. Pulse until they form a coarse crumb texture. Pick the thyme leaves off the woody stalks. Heat the olive oil in a large, deep, ovenproof skillet over medium–high heat. Add the bread/hazelnut mixture to the pan and cook for 2 minutes, stirring occasionally. Add the nutritional yeast and thyme leaves, season with salt and pepper and continue to cook for a couple of minutes until light golden. Transfer the crumbs to a bowl and wipe the pan clean.

Prep base. Slice the leeks into ¼in (5mm) thick rounds. Peel and grate the garlic. Zest the lemon. Open the cans of beans, then drain and discard about two-thirds of the liquid in each can.

Cook. Heat 4 tablespoons of olive oil in the skillet (make sure it is ovenproof) over medium heat. Add the leeks with a pinch of salt and fry for 7–8 minutes, stirring occasionally, until soft and starting to color. Add the garlic and lemon zest and cook for another 2 minutes. Pour the beans and their liquid into the pan with the mustard, miso, and nutritional yeast. Squeeze in the juice of the lemon and stir to combine. Simmer for a minute or two, stirring until the miso and mustard melt into the liquid. Add the peas and plant-based milk and simmer for 5–6 minutes, stirring occasionally, until heated through. Taste and season with salt and pepper.

Finish. Preheat the grill to high. Take the pan off the stove and sprinkle over the bread crumb mixture in an even layer. Put the pan under the preheated grill for a few minutes until the top is golden brown and crisp, keeping an eye out so the crumbs don't burn.

Assemble and serve. Spoon onto serving plates and enjoy!

STICKY DATE TEMPEH WOK-TOSSED NOODLES

PER PORTION:

- 8.75 PLANT POINTS
- 36g PROTEIN
- 853 kcal

Serves 2

For the chile vinegar
1 red chile
3 tbsp rice wine vinegar
½ tsp sugar
1 tbsp water

For the sticky date sauce
6oz (175g) pitted Medjool dates
2 in (5 cm) piece of fresh ginger
1 garlic clove
2 tbsp light (or dark) soy sauce
1 tbsp rice wine vinegar
1 tsp tamari
⅔ cup (150ml) water

For the stir-fry
7oz (200g) tempeh
7oz (200g) dried udon noodles (or 10oz/300g fresh, preferably whole wheat)
4 green onions
5½oz (150g) broccolini
5½oz (150g) shiitake mushrooms
1 carrot
1 red pepper
2 tbsp neutral oil of your choice
sea salt and freshly ground black pepper

To serve (optional)
roasted unsalted peanuts
cilantro leaves

Big flavors. Bold textures. Ultimate satisfaction. Caramelized, protein-rich tempeh, crisp vegetables, and chewy noodles come tossed in a glossy, sweet-savory sauce made with Medjool dates. Fresh herbs, a zingy chile vinegar, and peanuts for balance, heat, and crunch add the finishing touches. A seriously delicious dish.

Before you start: you will need a high-speed blender and a large wok (or deep skillet).

Make chile vinegar. Finely chop the chile and place in a bowl. Stir in the vinegar, sugar, and water. Set aside.

Make sauce. Roughly chop the dates. Peel and roughly chop the ginger and peel the garlic. Add the dates, ginger, and garlic to a blender with the soy sauce, vinegar, tamari, and water and blend until smooth. Taste and season with salt, if needed.

Marinate tempeh. Crumble the tempeh into ½ in (1 cm) chunks and add to a bowl with 2 tablespoons of the date sauce (set aside the rest for later), then stir to coat. Let marinate for 10 minutes.

Cook noodles. Cook the noodles following the package instructions, then drain and rinse under cold running water. Set aside.

Prep stir-fry. Meanwhile, slice the green onions into small pieces. Slice the broccolini in half lengthwise, then in half widthwise if thick. Cut the shiitake into ½ in (1 cm) slices. Slice the carrot into thin matchsticks and thinly slice the pepper, discarding the seedy core.

Stir-fry. Heat 1 tablespoon of the oil in a large wok over medium-high heat. Add the tempeh and stir-fry for 3–4 minutes, until golden. Remove to a bowl and wipe the wok clean. Add the remaining oil to the wok over high heat. Add the broccolini and shiitake and stir-fry for 2–3 minutes, until beginning to take on color. Add the green onions, carrot, and pepper and stir-fry for 2–3 minutes, until just tender. Add in the cooked noodles, tempeh, and the remaining sauce and cook for 2 minutes, stirring and tossing regularly. Taste and season with more soy sauce, salt, and pepper if needed.

Assemble and serve. Divide the stir-fry between bowls. Drizzle over the chile vinegar and top with peanuts and cilantro, if you like.

CHARRED MISO-BUTTER BROCCOLI (WITH ROMESCO BEANS)

PER PORTION:
- 8 PLANT POINTS
- 53g PROTEIN
- 1,290 kcal

Serves 2

For the miso-butter broccoli
1 large head of broccoli
3 tbsp plant-based butter
3 tbsp white miso
generous pinch of sea salt, plus extra to season

For the romesco beans
4 roasted red peppers in oil from a jar
1 garlic clove
1 x 15.5oz (439g) can cannellini beans
1 cup (150g) roasted almonds
1¼oz (35g) nutritional yeast
1 tbsp tomato paste
1 tbsp red wine vinegar
2 tsp sweet smoked paprika
freshly ground black pepper

For the lemon-tahini drizzle
1 lemon
2 tbsp tahini
3 tbsp water
salt

A flavor-packed dinner that feels special but doesn't take forever to make. Charred broccoli glazed in miso butter, served on a bed of smoky cannellini bean romesco, and finished with a zesty tahini drizzle. High in protein, full of fiber, and seriously satisfying—ideal for when you want something nourishing but a bit different.

Before you start: you will need a small saucepan, a high-speed blender, and a large griddle pan (or skillet). Line a medium roasting pan with parchment paper. Preheat the oven to 425°F (220°C).

Make miso-butter broccoli. Cut the broccoli head in half, then cut each half into 3 wedges, trim the stalks, and place in a lined roasting pan. Melt the plant-based butter with the miso in a small saucepan over low heat, stirring, until combined. Drizzle the miso butter over the broccoli and sprinkle with a generous pinch of salt. Roast in the preheated oven for 20–25 minutes, basting halfway through, until the broccoli is deep golden and slightly charred in places.

Make romesco beans. Meanwhile, drain the red peppers and peel the garlic and add to a blender. Drain the cannellini beans and add to the blender with the rest of the romesco ingredients and blend until smooth. Taste and season to perfection with salt and pepper. Set aside.

Make lemon-tahini drizzle. Squeeze the juice of 1 lemon into a small bowl. Add the tahini and water and whisk to combine, adding a splash more water to make a creamy consistency, if needed. Season with a little salt to taste.

Assemble and serve. Swirl a generous amount of the romesco beans onto each serving plate. Top with the charred broccoli, drizzling over any roasting juices in the pan. Spoon over the lemon-tahini drizzle to serve.

MAC 'N' BEANS

PER PORTION:
- 6 PLANT POINTS
- 36g PROTEIN
- 854 kcal

Serves 4

18oz (500g) macaroni, preferably whole wheat
1 tbsp white wine vinegar (or lemon juice)
handful of chives
"Bacon" Bits (see p220), to serve (optional)

For the crispy bread crumbs
2–3 slices of whole wheat sourdough bread
2 tbsp nutritional yeast
1 tbsp plant-based butter
sea salt and freshly ground black pepper

For the sauce
1 onion
2 garlic cloves
3 tbsp plant-based butter
pinch of sea salt
2 x 14oz (411g) cans lima beans
1¾oz (50g) nutritional yeast
2 tbsp Dijon mustard
2 tbsp white miso
1 tsp ground turmeric
½ tsp hot smoked paprika
1 cup (200ml) plant-based milk

A creamy, comforting twist on the classic mac and cheese, made with lima beans for a protein boost and silky texture. The sauce is rich, savory, and full of flavor with a crunchy sourdough topping for contrast. An easy, satisfying dish that delivers on taste and nutrition.

Before you start: you will need a food processor; a large, deep skillet; 2 large saucepans; and a high-speed blender.

Make and fry bread crumbs. Tear the bread into pieces and put it in a food processor with the nutritional yeast and pulse into chunky crumbs. Melt the butter in a large, deep skillet over medium–high heat. Add the crumbs, season with a little salt and pepper, and fry, stirring, until golden and crisp. Transfer to a bowl and set aside.

Prep sauce. Peel and finely dice the onion. Peel and grate the garlic. Melt the butter in a large pan over medium heat. Add the onion and a pinch of salt and fry for 5–6 minutes, stirring occasionally, until softened. Add the garlic and cook, stirring, for another minute. Add in the lima beans (with their liquid), stir to combine, and simmer for 2 minutes. Add the nutritional yeast, mustard, miso, turmeric, and smoked paprika; stir to combine and simmer for another minute. Stir in the milk and simmer for 2 minutes. Take the pan off the heat and let cool slightly.

Blend sauce. Transfer the contents of the pan to a blender and blend until smooth. Taste, season to perfection with salt and pepper, then return the sauce to the pan.

Cook pasta. Meanwhile, bring a separate large saucepan of salted water to a boil. Add the macaroni and cook according to the package instructions. Drain, reserving a cup of the cooking water.

Assemble and serve. Add the cooked macaroni to the sauce with the vinegar, and stir to combine, adding a splash of the pasta cooking water to loosen, if needed. Spoon the pasta into serving bowls, sprinkle with the bread crumbs and a sprinkling of chopped chives. Serve topped with "bacon" bits, if you like.

CAULIFLOWER STEAKS (WITH HARISSA LIMA BEAN MASH)

PER PORTION:
- **6 PLANT POINTS**
- **16.5g PROTEIN**
- **593 kcal**

Serves 2

1 cauliflower
2 tsp ground cumin
2 tsp ground cilantro
2 tsp hot smoked paprika
2 tsp sea salt, plus extra to season
1 tsp freshly ground black pepper, plus extra to season
4 tbsp olive oil
2 tbsp maple (or agave) syrup
3 tbsp water

For the harissa lima bean mash
1 x 14oz (411g) can lima beans
2 tbsp olive oil
2 tbsp harissa paste

To serve
parsley leaves
mixed seeds or Protein Packed seed blend (see p208)
Fresh Green Drizzle (see p216)

A bold and satisfying dish made from simple, nourishing ingredients. Spiced, caramelized cauliflower steaks sit on a bed of creamy mash made from lima beans and cauliflower, infused with smoky harissa. Using the remaining cauliflower to make "steaks" means nothing goes to waste. It comes with a vibrant green drizzle and a topping of seeds and herbs for texture and zing; this one's a real showstopper.

Before you start: you will need a large saucepan, a high-speed blender, and a skillet. Line a medium baking sheet with parchment paper. Preheat the oven to 425°F (220°C).

Prep cauliflower. Remove the cauliflower leaves and trim the main stalk so the base is neat. Cut a thick slice, the same width as the stalk, out of the middle section of the cauliflower. Carefully cut the slice in half lengthwise to create two "steaks." Set the remaining cauliflower aside.

Roast cauliflower. Add the cumin, ground cilantro, smoked paprika, salt, pepper, olive oil, and maple syrup to a small bowl with the water and stir to combine. Brush the marinade over both sides of the "steaks" and place on a lined baking sheet. Roast the cauliflower for 25 minutes, turning halfway, until tender.

Prep mash. Meanwhile, roughly chop the remaining cauliflower. Cook in a large saucepan of boiling salted water for 10–12 minutes, until very tender, then drain and let cool for a few minutes. Add the cauliflower and drained lima beans to a blender and blend until smooth (add a splash of water to get a nice, creamy consistency).

Finish mash. Warm the olive oil and harissa in a skillet over medium heat. Add the blended lima bean and cauliflower mixture, stir to combine, and warm through until bubbling. Keep warm.

Assemble and serve. Transfer the mash to serving plates and smooth out with the back of a spoon. Top with the roasted cauliflower steaks, followed by the parsley and mixed seeds (or use the seed blend instead). Finish with the green drizzle and serve right away.

BIG BEET BURGERS

PER PORTION:

- **10.25 PLANT POINTS**
- **10.5g PROTEIN**
- **350 kcal**

Serves 4–6

1 sweet potato (about 5½–6oz/150–175g total weight)
10oz (300g) raw beets
3 tbsp olive oil, plus extra for drizzling over vegetables
1 onion
1 x 9oz (250g) package of ready-cooked brown rice
¼ cup (20g) coarse fresh whole wheat bread crumbs
½ tsp sea salt
½ tsp freshly ground black pepper
1 tsp ground cumin
1 tsp garlic powder
2 tsp hot smoked paprika
2 tbsp all-purpose flour
1 x 15oz (425g) can black beans

To serve
4–6 plant-based brioche burger buns
your favorite extras, such as plant-based mayo and ketchup, lettuce, tomato, pickles

Every now and then you just need a good burger. These patties are made with beets, sweet potato, black beans, and brown rice; packed with flavor, fiber, and natural goodness. They're perfect for loading up with your favorite sauces and toppings. Family-friendly, freezer-friendly, BBQ-friendly... delicious!

Before you start: you will need a large skillet and a food processor (or blender). Line a large baking sheet with parchment paper. Preheat the oven to 425°F (220°C).

Roast vegetables for patties. Peel the sweet potato and beets and cut them into ½ in (1 cm) cubes. Put them on a lined baking sheet, drizzle over some olive oil, and roast for 18–20 minutes, until tender. Take them out of the oven and set aside, reserving the lined tray.

Prep onion. Meanwhile, peel and finely dice the onion. Heat 1 tablespoon of the olive oil in a large skillet over medium heat and fry the onion for 10–15 minutes, until very soft. Transfer the onion to a large bowl and give the pan a wipe.

Blend patty mixture. Put the roasted vegetables in a food processor along with the cooked rice, bread crumbs, salt, pepper, ground cumin, garlic powder, smoked paprika, and flour. Drain and add the black beans, then blend into a thick paste. Scrape the paste into the bowl with the onion and mix everything together.

Shape and cook patties. Divide the bean mixture into 4–6 even portions (depending on your desired size) and use your hands to shape each one into a patty. Add the remaining olive oil to the skillet set over medium-high heat. Fry the patties for 3 minutes on each side until golden. Transfer to the reserved lined tray and bake at 425°F (220°C) for 5 minutes, until golden brown and cooked through.

Assemble and serve. Toast both halves of each burger bun, if you prefer. Spread the base of the buns with your favorite sauces and layer up your burgers with all the extras. Top with the bun lid to serve.

BERRY'S SMASHED POTATOES (WITH BEET BEANS)

PER PORTION:
- 7.25 PLANT POINTS
- 18g PROTEIN
- 538 kcal

Serves 4

2¼lb (1kg) small new potatoes
olive oil, for drizzling

For the dill salt
2 tsp dried dill
1 tsp dried thyme
generous pinch of sea salt flakes

For the beet beans
2 x 15.5oz (439g) cans cannellini beans
3 cooked beets (not in vinegar)
1 garlic clove
6 tbsp tahini
½ tsp ground cumin
1 unwaxed lemon
splash of plant-based milk (or water), if needed
sea salt and freshly ground black pepper

For the toppings (optional)
plain plant-based yogurt
dill oil (or extra-virgin olive oi)
dill fronds
lemon zest

When we posted this on social media, it got millions of views. After a game of musical chairs one night, Henry and EmJ made it for their daughter Berry, who absolutely loved it! It's now a go-to in their house. A good source of protein and goodness, it makes a great meal for growing, healthy bodies.

Before you start: you will need a pestle and mortar (or high-speed blender) and a large baking sheet, lined with parchment paper (if using the oven). Preheat the air fryer to 400°F (200°C) or oven to 425°F (220°C).

Make dill salt. Add the dill, thyme, and salt to a pestle and mortar or blender and crush or blend to a powder. Set aside.

Prep potatoes. Place the potatoes in a large saucepan of salted cold water. Bring to a boil and cook for around 10 minutes, until tender but still holding together. Drain the potatoes and let steam-dry in the pan for a few minutes.

Air-fry potatoes. Put the potatoes onto a cutting board and carefully crush (without completely breaking them apart) with the bottom of a glass or the back of a fork. Drizzle with olive oil. Put in the preheated air fryer and cook for 15–20 minutes, until golden and crisp. (Alternatively, roast in the preheated oven on a lined baking sheet for 25 minutes, turning halfway.)

Make beet beans. Meanwhile, drain and rinse the cannellini beans and add to a blender with the beet, peeled garlic clove, tahini, and ground cumin. Squeeze in the juice of 1 lemon (save the zest for garnishing later) and blend until smooth and creamy, adding a splash of plant-based milk, if needed. Taste and season to perfection with salt and pepper.

Assemble and serve. Spoon the beet beans onto a serving dish or individual plates. Top with the crispy, smashed potatoes. Finish with a drizzle of yogurt, dill oil, dill fronds, and some grated lemon zest, if you like, and tuck in!

PICKLE BEAN-STUFFED BAKED POTATOES

PER PORTION:
- **9.25 PLANT POINTS**
- **37g PROTEIN**
- **700 kcal**

Serves 4

4 baking potatoes (about 9oz/250g each)
olive oil, for coating
2 tbsp plant-based butter
sea salt and freshly ground black pepper

For the pickle bean topping
7oz (200g) gherkins
¼ red onion
½ small cucumber
⅔ cup (25g) dill
1 lemon
1 x 15.5oz (439g) can cannellini beans
1 x 14oz (411g) can lima beans (or an extra can of cannellini)
16oz (450g) firm tofu
1oz (30g) nutritional yeast
1 tbsp extra-virgin olive oil
1 tbsp Dijon mustard
1 tbsp white wine vinegar
4 tbsp water

To serve
plant-based butter
whole cornichons

Crispy baked potatoes loaded with a creamy, tangy blend of tofu, beans, and pickles. Fresh dill and crunchy cornichons finish this simple, flavor-packed meal perfectly.

Before you start: you will need a high-speed blender (or food processor). Preheat the air fryer to 425°F (220°C) or oven to 475°F (240°C).

Cook potatoes. Prick the potatoes 5–6 times all over with a fork, then microwave for 20 minutes, turning every 5 minutes. Rub the potatoes in olive oil and season generously with salt. Cook the potatoes in the preheated air fryer for 10 minutes (or bake on the top shelf of a preheated oven), until tender on the inside, and golden and crisp on the outside. Test with a sharp knife to make sure the potatoes are cooked all the way through.

Prep pickle beans. Meanwhile, finely chop the gherkins, onion, and cucumber, then set aside. Chop the dill fronds and set aside. Juice the lemon. Drain and rinse the cannellini and lima beans.

Blend filling base. Drain the tofu and put it into a blender with the canned beans, nutritional yeast, lemon juice, olive oil, mustard, and vinegar. Pour in the water and blend for about 2 minutes, until smooth and thick, adding a little more water if needed. Season generously with salt and pepper.

Combine. Transfer the creamy tofu mixture to a bowl and fold in three-quarters of the chopped gherkins, onion, cucumber, and dill (saving the rest to serve). Taste and adjust the seasoning with salt and pepper, if needed.

Assemble and serve. Cut each potato in half, fluff up the insides, and add a knob of plant-based butter. Spoon the pickle beans on top, then sprinkle over the whole cornichons and the reserved gherkins, onion, cucumber, and dill to serve.

KIMCHI RICE
(WITH GOCHU-CAULI WEDGES)

PER PORTION:

- **9.5 PLANT POINTS**
- **23.5g PROTEIN**
- **812 kcal**

Serves 2

For the gochu-cauli wedges
1 small cauliflower
2 tbsp gochujang
2 tbsp light soy sauce (or tamari)
1 tbsp maple (or agave) syrup
1 tbsp rice wine vinegar
1 tsp toasted sesame oil
1 tbsp neutral oil of your choice

For the kimchi rice
4¼oz (120g) kimchi
1 small red onion
2 green onions
1 in (2.5 cm) piece of fresh ginger
2 garlic cloves
¾ cup (150g) long-grain rice
1 tbsp neutral oil of your choice
1 tsp toasted sesame oil
pinch of salt, plus extra to season
1¼ cups (300ml) vegetable stock

For the peanut drizzle
3 tbsp (50g) peanut butter, smooth or crunchy
1 tbsp maple (or agave) syrup
1 tbsp light soy sauce (or tamari)
1 tbsp red wine vinegar
freshly ground black pepper

To serve
cilantro leaves
roasted unsalted peanuts
1 lime

Spicy, sticky cauliflower wedges on a bed of kimchi-studded rice, then finished with a zingy peanut drizzle. This is bold, satisfying comfort food with a bit of crunch and kick.

Before you start: you will need a large baking sheet and a medium saucepan with lid. Preheat the oven to 425°F (220°C).

Prep and marinate cauliflower. Remove the outer leaves and cut the cauliflower into 6 chunky wedges (through the core so they hold together). In a bowl, mix together the gochujang, soy sauce, maple syrup, vinegar, sesame oil, and oil. Brush or rub the marinade all over the cauliflower wedges, coating them thoroughly. Set aside.

Bake cauliflower wedges. Arrange the cauliflower wedges on the baking sheet and roast in the preheated oven for 25 minutes, until nicely golden and cooked through.

Prep kimchi rice. Meanwhile, roughly chop the kimchi and peel and slice the onion into thin wedges. Finely chop the green onions, keeping the white and green parts separate. Peel and grate the ginger and garlic. Rinse the rice in a sieve until the water runs clear.

Cook kimchi rice. Heat 1 tablespoon of oil in a medium saucepan over medium heat. Add the onion and cook for 5 minutes, until softened. Stir in the white part of the green onions, ginger, and garlic, and cook for another minute, until fragrant. Add the kimchi and stir until caramelized slightly. Add the rice with a pinch of salt, stir to coat it in the flavorings, then pour in the stock. Bring up to a boil, then cover with the lid and turn the heat down to the lowest setting. Cook the rice for 12–15 minutes, until tender and the water has been absorbed. Remove the pan from the heat and let stand for 5 minutes, then fluff up the rice with a fork.

Make peanut drizzle. Meanwhile, whisk together the peanut drizzle ingredients with 1 tablespoon water in a small bowl. Taste and add a splash more vinegar, if needed, and season with salt and pepper.

Assemble and serve. Spoon the kimchi rice into serving bowls, top with the cauliflower and the peanut drizzle. Sprinkle over the green part of the green onions, some chopped cilantro leaves,q and chopped peanuts. Cut the lime into wedges and serve on the side.

SMOKY BBQ PULLED OYSTER MUSHROOM TACOS

PER PORTION:

- 7 PLANT POINTS
- 29g PROTEIN
- 781 kcal

Serves 2

For the pulled mushrooms

1lb 5oz (600g) oyster mushrooms
2 tbsp olive oil
½ tsp cayenne pepper (you can increase amount to 1–2 tsp, depending on spice preference)
2 tbsp light soy sauce
2 tsp liquid smoke (optional)
1 tbsp hot (or sweet) smoked paprika
2 tsp dried oregano
1 tsp ground cumin
1 tbsp maple (or agave) syrup
3 tbsp nutritional yeast
sea salt and freshly ground black pepper

For the salsa

2 large tomatoes
½ red onion
1 green jalapeño chile
2 ripe peaches
1 handful of cilantro
2 tsp olive oil
1 tbsp lime juice, plus extra, if needed

To serve

6 soft corn tortillas
Fresh Green Drizzle (see p216), optional
1 lime

Super smoky and satisfyingly spicy, these tacos have a real wow-factor. Meaty mushrooms, refreshing salsa, and silky drizzle will have you wishing it was Taco Tuesday everyday.

Before you start: you will need a small skillet. Line a large baking sheet with parchment paper (if using the oven). Preheat the air fryer to 350°F (180°C) or oven to 400°F (200°C).

Prep mushrooms. Using your fingers, pull the oyster mushrooms into ½–¾ in (1–2 cm) long strips. Mix together the oil and all the seasonings in a large bowl to make a marinade. Season with salt and pepper. Add the pulled mushrooms and toss them in the marinade until well coated.

Cook mushrooms. Put the marinated mushrooms into the preheated air fryer and cook for 10–12 minutes, tossing them halfway through, until golden and slightly charred at the edges. (Alternatively, cook in the preheated oven on a lined baking sheet for 20–25 minutes, turning halfway through.)

Make salsa. Meanwhile, dice the tomatoes and finely chop the onion, jalapeño, and cilantro leaves and stalks (saving some of the leaves to garnish). Pit the peaches and finely chop the fruit. Add all the salsa ingredients to a bowl and stir to combine. Taste and season with salt, pepper, and more lime juice, if desired.

Warm tortillas. Warm the tortillas, one at a time, in a dry skillet over high heat (or you can use a microwave). Continue to warm the rest of the tortillas, stacking them under a clean dish towel to keep them warm and soft until ready to assemble.

Assemble and serve. Serve family-style, letting everyone help themselves, or spoon your mushrooms onto the warm tortillas and add a spoonful or two of the salsa on top of each. Finish with the green drizzle, if using, a wedge of lime, and the reserved cilantro.

ROASTED BEAN & EGGPLANT TABBOULEH

PER PORTION:
- **11.5 PLANT POINTS**
- **6.5g PROTEIN**
- **316 kcal**

Serves 4

1 eggplant
1 red onion
1 zucchini
1 red pepper
1 x 15.5oz (400g) can lima beans
2 tbsp olive oil
1 tbsp ground cumin
1 tbsp sweet smoked paprika
sea salt and freshly ground black pepper

For the couscous
7oz (200g) whole grain couscous
1 unwaxed lemon
handful of raisins (or chopped dried apricots)
pinch of sea salt
1 cup (225ml) hot vegetable stock
½ cup (20g) parsley leaves
½ cup (20g) mint leaves
1 cup (100g) pomegranate seeds

To serve
All Day Ranch Drizzle or Sun-dried Tomato Drizzle (see pp217–18)
sumac

Not your traditional tabbouleh. Roasted spiced vegetables and beans, herby couscous, and sweet pops of pomegranate, and your favorite drizzle. Fresh, hearty, and full of flavor!

Before you start: line a large baking sheet with parchment paper. Preheat the oven to 425°F (220°C).

Prep ingredients. Dice the eggplant, onion, zucchini, and red pepper, discarding the seedy core, into ¾ in (2 cm) chunks. Drain and rinse the lima beans, then pat dry with paper towels.

Roast vegetables and beans. Spread the vegetables and beans out on a lined baking sheet. Drizzle with 1 tablespoon of the olive oil and sprinkle over the ground cumin and smoked paprika. Season with salt and pepper, then toss the vegetables and beans to coat them in the spiced oil. Roast in the oven for 25–30 minutes, until golden and beginning to crisp.

Make couscous. Meanwhile, add the couscous to a heatproof bowl. Finely grate the lemon zest and add to the bowl with the raisins and a pinch of salt. Pour over the hot stock, cover with a plate, and leave for 5 minutes, or until the stock is absorbed. Fluff up the couscous with a fork, squeeze in the lemon juice, and add the remaining 1 tablespoon of olive oil, the herbs, and pomegranate seeds. (Save some of the herbs, and pomegranate to garnish at the end.)

Assemble and serve. Spoon the couscous onto a large serving plate. Top with the roasted vegetables and beans. Spoon (or squeeze) over your choice of drizzle, sprinkle with a little sumac, and finish with a sprinkling of herbs and pomegranate seeds, to serve.

KEBAB
(WITH HIGH-PROTEIN FLATBREADS)

PER PORTION:

- 6.75 PLANT POINTS
- 39g PROTEIN
- 654 kcal

Serves 4

For the tofu kebab "meat"
12oz (350g) extra-firm tofu
1 tbsp olive oil
2 tsp light soy sauce
1 tsp maple (or agave) syrup
1 tsp sweet smoked paprika
1 tsp garlic powder
1 tsp onion powder
1 tsp ground cumin
½ tsp cayenne pepper
pinch of freshly ground black pepper

For the flatbreads
3 cups (375g) all-purpose flour, plus extra for dusting
2 tbsp nutritional yeast
1 tsp baking powder
pinch of sea salt
10oz (300g) silken tofu

For the extras
1 Baby Gem lettuce
2 tomatoes
1 cucumber
1 handful of mint leaves
1 handful of parsley leaves
few pickled chiles
plant-based yogurt (or garlic mayo)
your favorite chili sauce

Many moons ago we were partial to a Bossman kebab after a night out (if you know, you know). This alternative is much, much healthier and tastes just as good.

Before you start: you will need a large skillet. Line a large baking sheet with foil (if using the grill). Preheat the air fryer to 400°F (200°C) or grill to high.

Make flatbreads. Mix the flour, nutritional yeast, baking powder, and salt in a mixing bowl. Whisk (or blend) the silken tofu until smooth, then add to the flour mix. Add 3 tablespoons water and mix to a soft dough. Knead the dough on a lightly floured work surface for 2 minutes. Cover with a clean dish towel and let rest for 5 minutes. Divide the dough into 4 balls and let rest until ready to use.

Prep tofu. Meanwhile, drain the tofu and pat dry with paper towels to remove any excess moisture. Using a mandoline or sharp knife, slice the tofu into thin strips. Mix the olive oil, soy sauce, maple syrup, and all the spices in a mixing bowl. Add the tofu and toss gently to coat it in the marinade.

Cook tofu. Arrange the tofu in an even layer in the preheated air fryer and cook for 10 minutes, until crisped and slightly charred at the edges. Don't turn the tofu during cooking as you want one side crispy and the other soft to recreate a meaty texture. (If grilling the tofu, spread it on an oiled, lined baking sheet and place under a high grill for 10 minutes, watching closely to ensure it doesn't burn.)

Prep extras. Shred the lettuce and thinly slice the tomatoes. Slice the cucumber into ribbons and pick the mint and parsley leaves.

Cook flatbreads. Heat a large, dry skillet over high heat until hot. Roll each ball of dough into a round, about ⅛–¼ in (3–5 mm) thick. Place in the pan, one at a time, and cook for 1–2 minutes on each side until lightly golden. Once cooked, stack the flatbreads under a clean dish towel to keep warm and soft while you make the rest.

Assemble and serve. Top each warm flatbread with the tofu, sliced lettuce, tomato, cucumber, and pickled chiles. Drizzle over the sauces, sprinkle with the herbs,n and serve right away.

PEA & SPINACH RISOTTO (WITH MINT-FRIED PEAS)

PER PORTION:
- **5.25 PLANT POINTS**
- **26g PROTEIN**
- **690 kcal**

Serves 2

For the risotto
1 small onion
1 garlic clove
2½ tbsp olive oil
¾ cup (150g) Arborio rice
⅔ cup (150ml) white wine
2½ cups (600ml) hot vegetable stock
2 tbsp nutritional yeast
sea salt and freshly ground black pepper

For the pea & spinach cream
2½oz (75g) frozen peas
2½ cups (100g) spinach leaves
½ cup (20g) mint leaves
⅓ cup (100ml) hot vegetable stock (or water)

For the mint-fried peas
10 mint leaves
2½oz (75g) frozen peas
pinch of sea salt
1 tbsp nutritional yeast

To finish (optional)
drizzle of plant-based cream
mint leaves and/or pea tendrils

A vibrant twist on classic risotto with a creamy blend of peas, spinach, and fresh mint for color, health, and flavor. Topped with mint-fried peas, it's fresh, comforting, and full of goodness. Ideal for spring and summer—it really is a true reci-pea for success!

Before you start: you will need a high-speed blender; a large, deep skillet; and a small skillet.

Make pea & spinach cream. Place the peas, spinach, and mint in a blender, then pour in the hot stock and leave for a few minutes to allow the peas to defrost. When ready, blend until smooth and creamy, adding extra liquid if it's too thick. Set aside.

Start risotto. Peel and very finely chop the onion. Peel and mince the garlic. Heat 2 tablespoons of the olive oil in a large, deep skillet over medium heat. Add the onion and cook for 6–7 minutes, until softened and translucent but not browned. Add the garlic and risotto rice, and stir to combine. Cook for about 1 minute, until lightly toasted. Pour in the wine and cook until almost evaporated.

Add stock. Begin to add the hot vegetable stock to the pan, one ladleful at a time. Stir the rice frequently, letting it absorb most of the stock before adding the next ladleful. Continue to cook for 14–16 minutes, adding the rest of the stock, and until the rice is almost ready.

Add pea & spinach cream. Stir in the pea and spinach cream. Reduce the heat to low and let the risotto simmer for another 2–3 minutes, until the rice is cooked. Mix in the nutritional yeast, taste, and season with salt and pepper.

Fry minty peas. Thinly slice the mint leaves. Heat the remaining ½ tablespoon of olive oil in a small skillet over medium-high heat. Add the frozen peas and a pinch of salt and cook for 2–3 minutes, until warmed through. Stir in the nutritional yeast and mint for the final 30 seconds of cooking.

Assemble and serve. Spoon the risotto into bowls and swirl over a little plant-based cream if you want extra richness. Top with the mint-fried peas, then sprinkle with extra mint and/or pea tendrils for a burst of color and flavor, if you like.

HARISSA TEMPEH
(WITH LEMON & HERB PEARL COUSCOUS)

PER PORTION:
- **6.5 PLANT POINTS**
- **27g PROTEIN**
- **826 kcal**

Serves 2

2 shallots
2 garlic cloves
1 unwaxed lemon
3½oz (100g) Tuscan kale
3 tbsp olive oil
pinch of sea salt, plus extra to season
5½oz (150g) pearl couscous
2¼ cups (550ml) vegetable stock
1 cup (200ml) coconut cream
1 small handful of parsley leaves
1 small handful of dill fronds
freshly ground black pepper

For the harissa tempeh
7oz (200g) tempeh
2 tbsp harissa (apricot is preferred)
1 tsp light soft brown sugar

A bold, satisfying dish that balances sweet heat with creamy comfort. The sticky tempeh is packed with protein and coated in a harissa glaze, while the giant couscous is rich, lemony, and full of fresh herbs. Date night? Sorted!

Before you start: you will need a medium saucepan and a skillet with lid.

Prep couscous. Peel and finely dice the shallots. Peel and mince the garlic. Finely grate the zest of the lemon, then cut it in half, juice half and slice the other half into wedges. Remove the tough stalks from the Tuscan kale and thinly slice the leaves.

Cook couscous. Heat 1 tablespoon of the olive oil in a medium saucepan over medium heat. Add the shallots and a pinch of salt and cook for 6–7 minutes, stirring regularly, until softened but not browned. Add the couscous and stir to coat it in the oil and shallots. Pour in the stock and coconut cream, then cook for 10–12 minutes, or until the couscous is al dente. Top off with a splash of water if the couscous looks dry.

Prep and cook tempeh. Meanwhile, slice the tempeh into roughly ½in (1cm) thick discs. Heat the remaining 2 tablespoons of olive oil in the skillet over medium-high heat. Add the tempeh and fry for 2–3 minutes on each side, or until golden brown and crisp all over. Remove the tempeh from the pan onto a plate. Reduce the heat to low, add the harissa and brown sugar, and cook for a few minutes until sticky and fragrant. Return the tempeh to the pan and turn to coat it in the harissa sauce. Cover with a lid to keep the tempeh warm while you finish the couscous.

Finish couscous. Stir the kale leaves into the couscous and cook for 1–2 minutes, until wilted. Stir in the lemon zest and juice and most of the parsley and dill. Taste and season with salt and pepper, adding a little more water to the pan to loosen, if needed.

Assemble and serve. Divide the couscous between plates and top each serving with the harissa tempeh. Drizzle over any harissa juices in the pan and garnish with the remaining parsley and dill. Serve with the reserved lemon wedges for squeezing over, if liked.

ARUGULA, PEA & PISTACHIO PESTO LINGUINE

PER PORTION:

- 6.5 PLANT POINTS
- 34g PROTEIN
- 757 kcal

Serves 4

14oz (400g) linguine, preferably whole wheat

For the pesto

18oz (500g) frozen peas
¾ cup (100g) shelled, unsalted pistachios
1 unwaxed lemon
1 garlic clove
2 cups(50g) arugula
2 cups(50g) spinach leaves
1 cup (35g) basil, plus extra to garnish
1¾oz(50g) nutritional yeast
2 tbsp vegetable bouillon (or 1 vegetable stock pot)
¼ cup(50ml) extra-virgin olive oil
sea salt and freshly ground black pepper

A bright, punchy pasta with a protein-packed pesto that's creamy, zesty, and easy to make. Arugula, spinach, basil, pistachios, peas—this really is a green dream. Definitely one for your weekly repertoire!

Before you start: you will need a small skillet, a high-speed blender (or food processor), and a large saucepan.

Prep pesto. Pour boiling water over the peas in a heatproof bowl and let defrost for a few minutes, then drain. Meanwhile, heat a small skillet over medium heat until hot. Add the pistachios and toast for 2–3 minutes, tossing the pan occasionally, until the nuts are golden, then set aside to cool. Finely grate the lemon zest and squeeze the juice. Peel the garlic clove.

Blend pesto. Pour half of the peas and most of the pistachios (leaving some to garnish) into a blender. Add the remaining pesto ingredients, saving the lemon zest to garnish, and pulse to a coarse paste. Taste and season with salt and pepper, then set aside.

Cook pasta. Bring a large pan of salted water to a boil and cook the linguine according to the package instructions. Drain, reserving 1 cup (240ml) of the pasta cooking water.

Assemble and serve. Return the pasta to the pan with the reserved peas and pesto and toss well to combine, adding enough of the pasta cooking water to loosen. Give it one final taste and season with more nutritional yeast, salt, and pepper, if needed. Garnish with the lemon zest, extra basil, and the reserved pistachios, chopped, if you like.

ROASTED CHILE, TOMATO & CHICKPEA SPAGHETTI

PER PORTION:
- **6.25 PLANT POINTS**
- **37g PROTEIN**
- **995 kcal**

Serves 2

1 x 15oz (425g) can chickpeas
4 garlic cloves
1 red onion
5½oz (150g) sun-dried tomatoes in oil
1 red chile
18oz (500g) cherry tomatoes
1 tbsp tomato paste
1 tbsp fennel seeds
2 tbsp extra-virgin olive oil
9oz (250g) spaghetti, preferably whole wheat
1oz (25g) nutritional yeast
sea salt and freshly ground black pepper
handful of basil leaves
Crispy Tofu (see p224), to serve (optional)

Sweet cherry tomatoes, chunky golden chickpeas, and a good kick of chile, all roasted until jammy and tossed through spaghetti. Big flavors, simple ingredients, and very, very satisfying.

Before you start: you will need a large roasting pan and a large saucepan. Preheat the oven to 425°F (220°C).

Prep ingredients. Drain and rinse the chickpeas. Peel and finely slice the garlic. Peel and roughly chop the onion. Drain and finely chop the sun-dried tomatoes. Finely slice the red chile, discarding the seeds, if preferred.

Roast tomatoes and chickpeas. Add the chickpeas, garlic, onion, sun-dried tomatoes, chile, cherry tomatoes, tomato paste, and fennel seeds to the roasting pan. Stir to combine, drizzle with olive oil, and season generously with salt and pepper. Roast in the preheated oven for 20–25 minutes, until the tomatoes are blistered and jammy and the chickpeas are golden.

Cook pasta. Meanwhile, bring a large saucepan of salted water to a boil, add the spaghetti and cook according to the package instructions. Drain, reserving 1¼ cups (300ml) of the pasta cooking water.

Combine. Once the vegetables and chickpeas are roasted, pour half of the reserved pasta cooking water into the roasting pan and stir in the nutritional yeast. Add the drained spaghetti and toss well until combined, adding extra pasta water if it looks dry. Taste and season with more salt and pepper, if needed.

Assemble and serve. Divide the pasta, tomatoes, and chickpeas between bowls, sprinkle over some basil leaves, and serve topped with crispy tofu, if you like. Enjoy!

PLANT POINTS PAELLA
(WITH AIOLI)

PER PORTION:
- **11.5 PLANT POINTS**
- **15.5g PROTEIN**
- **647 kcal**

Serves 4

1 onion
10oz (300g) brown button mushrooms
1 carrot
1 red pepper
1 yellow pepper
2 garlic cloves
1 x 15.5oz (439g) can chickpeas
pinch of saffron threads (or 1 tsp ground turmeric)
2 tbsp olive oil, plus extra for drizzling
2 tbsp sweet smoked paprika
½ tsp cayenne pepper (optional)
1½ cups (300g) bomba rice for paella
1 x 14.5oz (411g) can diced tomatoes
7oz (200g) frozen peas
2 bay leaves
4 cups (1 liter) vegetable stock
sea salt and freshly ground black pepper
"Chorizo" Crumbles (see p222), to serve (optional)

For the aioli
1 large garlic bulb
¼ cup (75g) plant-based mayonnaise
1 lemon

Paella rice, chickpeas, peppers, and mushrooms come together in a richly spiced tomato broth, finished with a zingy squeeze of lemon and a creamy aioli. Big flavors, satisfying texture, and totally Instagram-worthy—a one-pan showstopper for you and the family.

Before you start: you will need a food processor and a large, deep skillet with lid.

Prep paella. In a food processor, blend the peeled onion, mushrooms, and carrot until finely chopped (or coarsely grate using a cheese grater). Slice the peppers, discarding the seedy cores. Peel and finely grate the garlic. Drain and rinse the chickpeas. Steep the saffron, if using, in 1 tablespoon hot water.

Start paella base. Heat the olive oil in a large, deep skillet. Add the onion, mushrooms, carrot, and peppers, and cook for 7–8 minutes, until soft, and the water from the mushrooms has evaporated. Add the smoked paprika, cayenne, and saffron, plus the soaking water (or add the turmeric at this point), and cook for another minute.

Cook paella. Stir the rice into the pan until coated in the vegetable mixture. Add the chickpeas, canned tomatoes, peas, bay leaves, and stock. Season generously with salt and pepper. Bring to a simmer, put the lid on, and cook for 15 minutes. Turn the stove off and leave the rice to steam-cook for another 5–10 minutes, or longer if needed, until the rice is tender with a little bite.

Make aioli. Meanwhile, trim the top of the garlic bulb, revealing a tiny bit of the cloves. Place the bulb in a microwave-safe container, add a drizzle of olive oil, a few tablespoons of water, and a little salt and pepper. Cover with the lid and microwave in 30-second blasts for 6–8 minutes, checking the garlic with the tip of a sharp knife until soft. Let cool, then squeeze out one half of the softened cloves and mash until smooth with the flat blade of a knife (save the remaining garlic for another dish). Stir the mashed garlic into the plant-based mayonnaise in a bowl. Squeeze in the juice of ½ lemon, stir and add 1 tablespoon water at a time until a creamy consistency.

Assemble and serve. Cut the remaining lemon into wedges. Serve the paella topped with the chorizo crumbles, if using, and drizzled with the aioli. Finish with wedges of lemon. Enjoy!

ONE-
POT/
PAN

SOUPER HEARTY RIBOLLITA

PER PORTION:

- **9.25 PLANT POINTS**
- **10.5g PROTEIN**
- **244 kcal**

Serves 6

1 onion
2 carrots
3 garlic cloves
2 celery stalks
2 x 15.5oz (439g) cans cannellini beans
2 Green Plant Point Cubes (see p215) or 3½oz (100g) kale or Tuscan kale leaves
2 tbsp extra-virgin olive oil
1 tsp dried thyme
1 rosemary sprig (or 1 tsp dried rosemary)
½ tsp chili flakes, plus extra to serve (optional)
2 tsp sweet smoked paprika
1 tbsp tomato paste
1 x 14.5oz (411g) can diced tomatoes
4 cups (1 liter) vegetable stock
5½oz (150g) day-old crusty bread, preferably whole wheat
¾oz (20g) nutritional yeast
1 tbsp lemon juice
sea salt and freshly ground black pepper
basil leaves, to garnish
"Bacon" Bits (see p220), to finish (optional)

This hearty Tuscan classic turns simple ingredients into something magical. Packed with beans, greens, and crusty bread, it's halfway between a soup and a stew. Filling, flavorful, and perfect for sharing.

Before you start: you will need a large saucepan (or pot) with lid.

Prep ingredients. Peel and finely chop the onion, carrots, and garlic. Finely chop the celery. Drain and rinse the cannellini beans. Remove and discard the stalks and roughly chop the kale leaves, if using.

Start soup. Heat 1 tablespoon of the olive oil in a large saucepan over medium heat. Add the onion, carrots, and celery, and cook for 7–8 minutes, until softened and the onion is turning golden. Add the garlic, thyme, rosemary, and chili flakes, if using, and cook for 1 minute, stirring, until fragrant. Stir in the smoked paprika and tomato paste and cook for another minute. Add the canned tomatoes, vegetable stock, and drained beans. Stir to combine, bring up to a boil, then turn the heat down to a simmer.

Thicken soup. Tear the bread into small pieces and add to the soup. Turn the heat down to low, cover with the lid, and simmer, stirring occasionally, for 15 minutes, until the bread breaks down and the soup thickens to a rustic, stewlike consistency.

Finish soup. Remove and discard the rosemary sprig, if using. Stir in the frozen green cubes or kale, if using, and cook until the cubes melt or the leaves wilt. Add the nutritional yeast and the lemon juice to balance the flavor. Taste and season with salt and plenty of black pepper. If the soup is too thick, add a splash of water, or if it's too thin, simmer, uncovered, for a few extra minutes.

Assemble and serve. Ladle the ribollita into bowls and drizzle each serving with the remaining olive oil. Sprinkle over some basil leaves and an extra pinch of chili flakes, if using. Finish with a sprinkling of "bacon" bits, if you like.

Store. Let the soup cool and store in the fridge for up to 3 days or freeze for up to 3 months.

GREEN TEMPEH YAKI UDON

PER PORTION:
- 7.5 PLANT POINTS
- 44g PROTEIN
- 889 kcal

Serves 2

5 green onions
3 garlic cloves
thumb-sized piece of fresh ginger
¼ green cabbage (about 7oz/200g)
5½oz (150g) beansprouts
5½oz (150g) frozen shelled edamame
2 tbsp neutral oil of your choice, plus extra if needed
7oz (200g) tempeh
pinch of sea salt
2 packets cooked thick udon noodles (around 14oz/400g total weight)
1 tbsp toasted sesame oil

For the yaki sauce
3 tbsp light soy sauce (or tamari)
2 tbsp mirin
1 tbsp coconut (or light soft brown) sugar
1 tbsp rice wine vinegar
2 tsp sriracha (or sambal oelek), optional

To serve
cilantro leaves
toasted sesame seeds

This stir-fried noodle dish is full of texture and bold flavor. Crispy, golden tempeh, crunchy vegetables, and thick udon noodles all tossed in a glossy, savory-sweet yaki sauce.

Before you start: you will need a large, nonstick skillet (or wok).

Prep ingredients. Trim and finely slice the green onions, separating the white and green parts. Peel and grate the garlic and ginger. Thinly slice the cabbage. Rinse the beansprouts. Put the edamame in a heatproof bowl, pour over just-boiled water to cover and let defrost.

Make yaki sauce. In a small bowl, mix the soy sauce, mirin, sugar, vinegar, and sriracha, if using, until the sugar dissolves. Set aside.

Cook tempeh. Heat the oil in a large, nonstick skillet over medium–high heat. Crumble in the tempeh in roughly ½ in (1 cm) pieces and season with a pinch of salt. Fry for 8–10 minutes, turning occasionally, until golden and crisp all over. Scoop the tempeh out of the pan onto a plate and set aside.

Cook vegetables. In the same pan, pour in a little more oil, if needed. Add the white part of the green onions and the garlic and ginger, then stir-fry for 1 minute, until fragrant. Add the cabbage and stir-fry for 3–4 minutes, until slightly softened. Drain and stir in the edamame and beansprouts and cook for another 2 minutes.

Add noodles and sauce. Add the udon noodles to the pan along with a splash of hot water to loosen and separate them. Gently toss together for 1 minute, until heated through.

Finish tempeh. Return the crispy tempeh to the pan and pour in the yaki sauce. Stir-fry for 2–3 minutes, until everything is glossy, hot and well coated. Stir in the sesame oil to finish.

Assemble and serve. Divide the vegetables and noodles between bowls. Chop the cilantro and sprinkle over with the sesame seeds and the reserved green part of the green onions. Serve hot and enjoy!

BIG BEAN JAMBALAYA

PER PORTION:
- **10.5 PLANT POINTS**
- **11.5g PROTEIN**
- **345 kcal**

Serves 6

2 onions
2 celery stalks
1 green pepper
1 red pepper
3 garlic cloves
1 x 15.5oz (439g) can kidney beans
1 x 15.5oz (439g) can lima beans (or cannellini beans)
3 tbsp olive oil
2 tsp sweet smoked paprika
2 tsp dried thyme
2 tsp dried oregano
1 tsp ground fennel
¼ tsp cayenne pepper
½ tsp freshly ground black pepper
1 bay leaf
1 tbsp tomato paste
1¼ cups (250g) long-grain rice
1 x 14.5oz (400g) can diced tomatoes
2 cups (500ml) fresh vegetable stock
sea salt

To serve
1 lemon
parsley leaves
hot sauce
"Chicken" Strips (see p221), to finish (optional)

Jambalaya is a Louisiana-born rice dish, big on flavor and full of comfort. This version is packed with beans, sweet peppers, and warming spices. Great for batch cooking or feeding a crowd.

Before you start: you will need a large casserole or saucepan with lid.

Prep ingredients. Peel and finely chop the onions and finely slice the celery. Dice the green and red peppers, discarding the seedy cores. Peel and mince the garlic. Drain the canned beans.

Cook base. Heat the oil in a large saucepan over medium heat. Add the onions, celery, and peppers, and cook for 5–6 minutes, until softened. Stir in the garlic, smoked paprika, thyme, oregano, fennel, cayenne pepper, pepper, and the bay leaf, and cook for 1 minute to release the flavor of the herbs and spices. Add the tomato paste and rice, then stir well to combine it with the seasoned oil and vegetables.

Simmer jambalaya. Pour the canned tomatoes, vegetable stock, and canned beans into the pan. Stir thoroughly, scraping the bottom of the pan to make sure nothing is sticking. Bring to a boil, then turn the heat down to low, cover with the lid, and simmer gently for about 15 minutes. Try not to stir the rice while it's cooking or it may turn mushy. Check the rice about halfway through, and if it looks dry, add a small splash of hot water, then quickly put the lid back on and continue to cook. Test a grain of rice to check it's cooked, then, if ready, gently fluff up the jambalaya with a fork. Taste and season with salt, if needed.

Assemble and serve. Cut the lemon into wedges and chop some parsley leaves. Serve the jambalaya in bowls with the lemon wedges for squeezing over. Sprinkle over the parsley and add a few dashes of hot sauce for a Louisiana-style kick. Finish with a topping of "chicken" strips, if you like.

Store. Let the jambalaya cool and store in the fridge for up to 2 days or freeze for up to 3 months. Reheat thoroughly before serving.

UNFRIED RICE

PER PORTION:
- **9.75 PLANT POINTS**
- **20g PROTEIN**
- **551 kcal**

Serves 4

9oz (250g) jasmine rice
1 in (2.5 cm) piece of fresh ginger
2 garlic cloves
3 green onions
3½oz (100g) smoked tofu (optional, for added protein)
18oz (500g) mixed stir-fry vegetables, such as carrots, sugar snap peas, cabbage, edamame, and sweet corn
1 tbsp vegetable oil
2 tbsp dark soy sauce
2 tsp white miso
2½ cups (600ml) vegetable stock
1 tbsp toasted sesame oil

For the green onion oil (optional)
2 green onions
1 in (2.5 cm) piece of fresh ginger
pinch of chili flakes (optional)
pinch of sea salt
3 tbsp neutral oil of your choice

To serve
1 lime
toasted sesame seeds
cilantro leaves
crispy chili oil (or sriracha), optional

All the flavor of fried rice, but none of the fuss. This one-pan dish simmers rice with vegetables, tofu, and umami-rich stock until tender, then finishes with a spicy topping and crunch.

Before you start: you will need a large, deep skillet with lid and a small saucepan (optional).

Prep ingredients. Rinse the rice in a sieve under cold running water until the water runs clear, then set aside. Peel and finely grate the ginger. Peel and finely chop the garlic. Trim and finely slice the green onions. Drain and pat dry the smoked tofu, if using, with paper towels to remove any excess water, then finely chop. Chop your stir-fry vegetables into bite-sized pieces, if needed.

Sauté vegetables and tofu. Heat 1 tablespoon of vegetable oil in a large, deep skillet over medium heat. Add the ginger, garlic, and green onions, and sauté for 2 minutes, until fragrant. Add the mixed vegetables and tofu, if using, then stir and cook for another 2–3 minutes, until the vegetables start to soften.

Build rice. Stir in the rice and let it toast for 1 minute. Add the soy sauce and miso, stirring until combined, then pour in the stock. Bring up to boiling, then turn the heat down to low and simmer gently, covered with a lid, for 12–15 minutes, until the rice is tender and the liquid is absorbed. Turn off the heat and let rice stand in the pan, with the lid on, for 5 minutes.

Make green onion oil (optional). Meanwhile, put the 2 green onions in a small heatproof bowl with the ginger, chili flakes, if using, and a pinch of salt. Heat the oil in a small saucepan until it starts to shimmer, then carefully pour it over the green onion mixture. Stir and set aside.

Assemble and serve. Fluff up the rice with a fork and drizzle over the sesame oil. Spoon the unfried rice into bowls and drizzle generously with the green onion oil, if using. Cut the lime into wedges. Finish the rice with a sprinkling of toasted sesame seeds and cilantro leaves and a drizzle of crispy chili oil (if not using the green onion oil), and with wedges of lime for squeezing over.

PILPELCHUMA CHICKPEA PILAF

PER PORTION:
- **7.25 PLANT POINTS**
- **16g PROTEIN**
- **634 kcal**

Serves 4

2 large onions
2 in (5 cm) piece of fresh ginger
25oz (700g) cooked chickpeas
3 tbsp olive oil
1½ cups (300g) basmati rice
3½ cups (825ml) vegetable stock
1 lemon, plus extra to serve (optional)
freshly ground black pepper

For the pilpelchuma paste
3 dried chipotle chiles
3 fresh red chiles, mild or hot, to taste
6 garlic cloves
1 tbsp sweet smoked paprika
2 tsp Aleppo chili flakes
2 tbsp tomato paste
4 tbsp olive oil
2 tsp light soft brown sugar
2 tsp sea salt, plus extra to season

To serve
toasted sliced almonds
cilantro leaves
1 lemon
"Chorizo" Crumbles (see p222), to finish (optional)

Sweet caramelized onions, fluffy spiced rice, and hearty chickpeas cooked in the fiery Libyan pilpelchuma chili paste. Great as a side for a crowd or a main with something fresh and crisp.

Before you start: you will need a high-speed blender (or food processor or spice grinder) and a large saucepan with lid.

Make pilpelchuma paste. Soak the chipotle chiles in a small bowl of hot water for about 10 minutes, until softened. Drain and remove the stems (and seeds if you prefer less heat). Place both types of chiles, the peeled garlic cloves, smoked paprika, chili flakes, tomato paste, olive oil, sugar, and salt into a blender and blend until smooth, scraping down the sides, if needed. Spoon into an airtight container and set aside. (It will keep stored in the fridge for up to 2 weeks.)

Prep pilaf ingredients. Meanwhile, peel and finely dice the onions and ginger. Drain the chickpeas.

Make pilaf base. Heat the olive oil in a large saucepan over high heat. Add the onions with a little salt and cook, stirring, for 5 minutes, until golden. Add the ginger and 3 tablespoons of the pilpelchuma paste and cook for 1 minute, until fragrant. Stir in the chickpeas and rice until coated in the spicy oil.

Simmer pilaf. Stir in the stock, scraping the bottom of the pan to make sure nothing is sticking. Bring to a boil, then turn the heat down to low, cover with the lid, and simmer gently for about 15 minutes, until the rice is tender and the liquid po is absorbed. Turn off the heat, squeeze in the juice of 1 lemon and let the rice to stand, covered, for 5 minutes. Gently fluff up the rice with a fork and season with salt and pepper, to taste.

Assemble and serve. Spoon the pilaf into bowls. Garnish with toasted sliced almonds and plenty of roughly chopped cilantro leaves. For extra zing, serve with lemon wedges for squeezing over. Sprinkle over the "chorizo" crumbles for a protein boost, if you like.

HARISSA SWEET POTATO SOUP

PER PORTION:

- 10.75 PLANT POINTS
- 13 PROTEIN
- 427 kcal

Serves about 4

1 onion
2 garlic cloves
21oz (600g) sweet potatoes (about 2)
1 large carrot
1 red pepper
1 lemon
3½oz (100g) split red lentils
2 tbsp olive oil
2 tbsp harissa paste
1 tbsp tomato paste
1 tsp ground cumin
7¼ cups (1.75 liters) vegetable stock
2 cups (60g) baby spinach (or kale) leaves
1oz (25g) nutritional yeast
freshly ground black pepper

For the lemon harissa yogurt
7oz (200g) coconut yogurt
1 lemon
2 tsp harissa paste
pinch of sea salt, plus extra to season

To serve
cilantro leaves
toasted pumpkin seeds

This one reminds us of Lily, our former head of food and the queen of harissa. Velvety sweet potato and lentils, zingy yogurt on top. Bright, bold, deeply comforting. Yum.

Before you start: you will need a large saucepan (or pot) and an immersion blender (or high-speed blender).

Prep ingredients. Peel and finely chop the onion and garlic. Peel the sweet potatoes and carrot and chop them into chunks. Chop the red pepper, discarding the seedy core. Squeeze the juice of the lemon into a bowl. Rinse the lentils well in a sieve under cold running water, until the water runs clear, then let drain.

Start soup. Heat the olive oil in a large saucepan over medium heat. Add the onion and garlic and sauté for 5 minutes, until softened. Stir in the harissa, tomato paste, and ground cumin, and cook for 1 minute, stirring, until fragrant. Add the carrot, sweet potatoes, and red pepper, then pour in the vegetable stock and add in the red lentils. Bring to a boil, then reduce the heat and simmer, stirring occasionally, for 15–20 minutes, until the sweet potato, carrot, and lentils are very tender.

Make lemon harissa yogurt. Meanwhile, mix all the ingredients for the lemon harissa yogurt together in a bowl and set aside.

Blend soup. Using an immersion blender (or you can use a regular blender but let the soup cool slightly first), blend the soup until smooth and creamy.

Finish soup. Return the pan to low heat to heat the soup through, adding a little water if the soup is too thick. Stir in the spinach and let the leaves wilt in the hot soup. Add the nutritional yeast, and season with salt and pepper to taste.

Assemble and serve. Ladle the soup into bowls and swirl a spoonful of the harissa yogurt on top of each serving. Sprinkle a few cilantro leaves and toasted pumpkin seeds over to serve.

Store. Let the soup cool and store in the fridge for up to 3 days or freeze for up to 3 months.

GREEN MINESTRONE "STEWP"

PER PORTION:
- 15 PLANT POINTS
- 21g PROTEIN
- 535 kcal

Serves 6

1 onion
1 leek
1 celery stalk
2 garlic cloves
7oz (200g) green beans
3½oz (100g) snow peas
1 zucchini
3½oz (100g) kale
1 unwaxed lemon
1 x 15.5oz (439g) can cannellini beans
2 tbsp olive oil
¼ tsp chili flakes, plus extra to serve
10oz (300g) ditalini (or orzo)
7½ cups (1.8 liters) vegetable stock
2 Green Plant Point Cubes (see p215) or 2½ cups (80g) baby spinach leaves
5½oz (150g) frozen peas
freshly ground black pepper

For the pesto
1½ cups (25g) mint leaves, plus extra to serve
1½ cups (25g) parsley leaves, plus extra to serve
1½ cups (25g) basil leaves, plus extra to serve
1 unwaxed lemon
1¼oz (35g) nutritional yeast, plus extra to serve
½ cup (50g) pistachios (or pine nuts)
⅓ cup (100ml) extra-virgin olive oil
pinch of sea salt, plus extra to season

A bit like a soup, a bit like a stew—that's why we call it a "stewp." Stewpid? Maybe. Delicious? Definitely. Packed with green vegetables, pasta, and pesto, it's fresh, hearty, and full of flavor.

Before you start: you will need a high-speed blender (or food processor) and a large saucepan (or pot).

Make pesto. Pick the mint, parsley, and basil leaves and finely slice the stalks. Zest and juice the lemon. Place the herb leaves, nutritional yeast, pistachios, and lemon zest into a blender. Pour in the lemon juice and olive oil, add a pinch of salt and pulse to a chunky green pesto, scraping down the sides, if needed. Set aside.

Prep vegetables. Peel and dice the onion. Thinly slice the leek and celery, and peel and grate the garlic. Trim the green beans and cut into bite-sized pieces. Trim the snow peas. Finely dice the zucchini. Strip and roughly chop the kale leaves, discarding the tough stalks. Zest and juice the lemon. Drain and rinse the cannellini beans.

Start "stewp." Heat the olive oil in a large pan over medium–high heat. Add the onion, leek, celery, zucchini, and some salt and cook for 8 minutes, until softened. Add the garlic and chili flakes and cook for 1 minute, until fragrant. Pour in the vegetable stock, then bring to a gentle boil over medium heat. Add the green cubes (if using spinach, add a bit later), then stir and heat through.

Finish "stewp." Add the pasta and cannellini beans to the pan. Stir well, reduce the heat slightly and simmer for 5 minutes to start cooking the pasta, then add the green beans, snow peas, kale, spinach, and peas, if not using the green cubes. Stir well and simmer for another 3 minutes, or until the pasta is al dente and the vegetables are tender but still bright green. Turn off the heat and stir through 2 tablespoons of the pesto. Add the remaining lemon juice, to taste (you may not want to use all of it). Season to taste.

Assemble and serve. Ladle the soup into serving bowls. Top with a the pesto, extra nutritional yeast, chili flakes, and reserved lemon zest. Garnish with a few extra herbs before serving.

Store. Leave the soup to cool and store in the fridge for up to 3 days or freeze for up to 3 months.

ROASTED HARISSA CHICKPEAS

PER PORTION:
- **8 PLANT POINTS**
- **17g PROTEIN**
- **434 kcal**

Serves 2

1 Romano pepper
7oz (200g) good-quality cherry tomatoes
25oz (700g) cooked chickpeas
2 tbsp olive oil, plus extra to serve
good pinch each of sea salt and freshly ground black pepper, plus extra to season
2 tbsp rose harissa paste, plus extra to serve
1 x 14.5oz (411g) can diced tomatoes
pinch of sugar, to taste
2½ cups(75g) baby spinach leaves
1 lemon

To serve
hummus
parsley leaves
pine nuts
slices of sourdough, preferably whole wheat

A cozy, vibrant bowl full of warmth and flavor. Jammy harissa chickpeas, blistered tomatoes, creamy hummus, and lemon. Best served with crunchy toast for dunking.

Before you start: you will need a large baking dish. Preheat the oven to 425°F (220°C).

Prep ingredients. Halve the Romano pepper, remove the seeds and finely slice. Halve the cherry tomatoes. Drain the chickpeas.

Roast. Put the pepper and tomatoes into a large baking dish, drizzle over the olive oil and season with a good pinch each of salt and pepper. Shake the pan to coat the tomatoes and pepper in the seasoned oil. Put the pan in the preheated oven and roast for 10 minutes. Stir in the harissa, canned tomatoes, chickpeas, and a pinch of sugar. Return the pan to the oven for a further 20 minutes, until the sauce is reduced and jammy.

To finish. When ready, remove the pan from the oven, stir in the spinach and let stand briefly until the leaves wilt. Cut the lemon in half and squeeze the juice from one half into the pan. Cut the other half into wedges and set aside to serve. Taste and season with salt and pepper.

Assemble and serve. Dollop the hummus on top of the pan and swirl it into the roasted chickpea mixture. Mix a little extra harissa paste with some olive oil and drizzle it over. Chop the parsley and sprinkle over with the pine nuts. Serve with slices of sourdough (buttered and toasted) and the remaining lemon wedges for squeezing over.

Store. Let the roasted harissa chickpeas cool and store in the fridge for up to 3 days or freeze for up to 3 months.

LODGE

CREAMY LEEK & LIMA BEAN PHYLLO PIE

PER PORTION:

- **8.25 PLANT POINTS**
- **20g PROTEIN**
- **572 kcal**

Serves 4

For the filling
3 large leeks
3 garlic cloves
1 unwaxed lemon
2 x 15.5oz (439g) cans lima beans
2 tbsp olive oil
pinch of sea salt, plus extra to season
2 tsp dried thyme
2 tbsp all-purpose flour
1 cup (250ml) vegetable stock
1 x 13.5oz (400ml) can coconut milk
2 tbsp white miso
2 tbsp nutritional yeast, optional, for extra savory flavor
3¼ cups (100g) baby spinach leaves
freshly ground black pepper

For the phyllo topping
4–5 sheets plant-based phyllo pastry
2 tbsp olive oil
1 tbsp fennel seeds

To serve
parsley leaves
salad or seasonal greens

This golden phyllo pie is creamy, savory, and full of goodness. The leeks, beans, and coconut milk make the filling rich and comforting, with crisp phyllo pastry on top for a satisfying crunch.

Before you start: you will need a large, deep, ovenproof skillet. Preheat the oven to 425°F (220°C).

Prep filling ingredients. Finely slice the leeks. Peel and mince the garlic. Zest and juice the lemon. Drain and rinse the lima beans.

Cook filling base. Heat the olive oil in a large, deep, ovenproof pan over medium heat. Add the leeks and a pinch of salt and cook for 5 minutes, stirring often, until soft and translucent. Add the garlic and thyme and cook for another minute.

Build sauce. Add the flour and cook for 1 minute, stirring. Gradually, pour in the stock, stirring to avoid any lumps forming. Add the coconut milk, miso, and nutritional yeast, if using, then season with salt and pepper. Simmer the sauce for 5 minutes, until smooth and thickened. Add in the lima beans and spinach, stir, and cook until the leaves wilt and the beans are heated through. Add the lemon juice and zest. Taste and season with extra salt and pepper, if needed.

Top pie. Remove the pan from the heat. Scrunch each sheet of phyllo loosely and arrange them over the filling until they cover the top. Brush or spray with olive oil and sprinkle with fennel seeds.

Bake pie. Transfer the pan to the preheated oven and bake for 18 minutes, until the phyllo is crisp and golden.

Assemble and serve. Chop the parsley and sprinkle over the top of the pie before serving with a salad or seasonal greens on the side.

SHEET PAN HARISSA TOFU AND VEGGIES

PER PORTION:

- 11.25 PLANT POINTS
- 27g PROTEIN
- 465 kcal

Serves 6

For the harissa marinade
3 garlic cloves
3 tbsp harissa paste
3 tbsp olive oil
1 tbsp lemon juice
2 tbsp maple (or agave) syrup
½ tsp sea salt
½ tsp freshly ground black pepper

For the sheet pan
20oz (560g) firm tofu
1 large red pepper
1 large yellow pepper
2 red onions
1 zucchini
1 x 15oz (425g) can chickpeas
7oz (200g) cherry tomatoes
2 lemons

For the cashew cream
1 cup (150g) raw cashews
⅔ cup (140ml) plant-based milk
1oz (25g) nutritional yeast
½ tsp sea salt

To serve
cilantro leaves
pomegranate seeds

This easy sheet pan meal is bold, bright, and full of flavor. Harissa-roasted tofu and veggies meet creamy cashew sauce, with bursts of pomegranate and fresh herbs to bring it all together.

Before you start: you will need a high-speed blender. Line 2 large baking sheets with parchment paper. Preheat the oven to 425°F (220°C).

Prep harissa marinade. Peel and crush the garlic, then combine with the harissa, olive oil, lemon juice, maple syrup, salt, and pepper in a large bowl.

Prep sheet pan. Drain the tofu and pat dry with paper towels to remove any excess moisture. Tear the tofu into bite-sized chunks and add to the marinade. Cut the red and yellow peppers into similar-sized chunks, discarding the seedy cores. Peel and cut the onions into thick wedges. Slice the zucchini into thick half-moons. Drain the chickpeas. Add the prepared vegetables to the marinade with the chickpeas and cherry tomatoes and toss well to combine.

Start sheet pan. Divide the marinated tofu and vegetables between 2 lined baking sheets, spreading them out in an even layer. Halve the lemons, then make space in both pans, adding them cut-side down. Roast in the preheated oven for 30 minutes, swapping the pans halfway, until the tofu is golden and the vegetables are tender.

Start cashew cream. Meanwhile, place the cashews in a heatproof bowl, pour over enough just-boiled water to cover and let soften for at least 10 minutes. Drain and blend the nuts in a blender with the rest of the cashew cream ingredients until smooth.

Finish cashew cream. Once the sheet pan is ready, let the lemon halves cool a little, then squeeze the juice into the cashew cream. Stir and season with extra salt and some pepper, if needed.

Assemble and serve. Spoon the tofu and vegetables onto plates and drizzle over the cashew cream. Sprinkle over some chopped cilantro leaves and pomegranate seeds. Any leftovers can be stored in the fridge for up to 4 days.

BISH BATCH BOSH!

MORE PLANTS SIGNATURE SOUP

PER PORTION:
- **13.75 PLANT POINTS**
- **7.5g PROTEIN**
- **140 kcal**

Serves about 6

2 carrots
2 leeks
2 celery stalks
3 garlic cloves
1 head of broccoli
2 zucchini
3½oz (100g) green beans
2 tbsp olive oil
5 cups (1.2 liters) vegetable stock
3½oz (100g) kale leaves
5½oz (150g) frozen peas
5½oz (150g) spinach leaves
2 unwaxed lemons
1½ cups (25g) basil leaves (or parsley)
1oz (30g) nutritional yeast
sea salt and freshly ground black pepper

To serve
Pesto Drizzle (see p217) or Romesco Drizzle (see p216) or use a store-bought alternative
Protein Packed seed blend (see p208) or mixed seeds
herb oil (or extra-virgin olive oil)

Here it is... a soup so good, we named it after the book you're holding. Full of greens, herbs, and plant points, it's smooth, zesty, and seriously cockle-warming.

Before you start: you will need a large saucepan and an immersion blender (or high-speed blender).

Prep vegetables. Finely chop the carrots, leeks, and celery. Peel and grate the garlic. Chop the broccoli and zucchini into small ¾ in (2 cm) chunks. Trim the green beans.

Cook base. Heat the olive oil in a large saucepan over medium heat. Add the carrots, leeks, and celery, and cook for 10–12 minutes, until softened. Add the garlic and cook for another minute.

Add vegetables and simmer. Add the broccoli, zucchini, green beans, and stock to the pan. Stir and bring up to a boil, then turn the heat down and simmer for 10 minutes. Add the kale and peas and simmer for another 5 minutes. Stir in the spinach and cook briefly until wilted, then remove the pan from the heat.

Blend. Juice the lemons (saving some of the zest to garnish) and add to the soup with the basil and nutritional yeast. Using an immersion blender (or transfer the soup to a blender in batches), blend until smooth. Stir and season with salt and pepper.

Assemble and serve. Ladle the soup into bowls and swirl over your choice of drizzle or use a store-bought alternative. Top with the seeds, herb oil, and the reserved lemon zest to serve.

Store. If not serving right away, divide the soup into portions and let cool. Store in the fridge for up to 4 days or freeze for up to 3 months.

CHARRED EGGPLANT & BLACK BEAN BOWL

PER PORTION:
- **12.75 PLANT POINTS**
- **22g PROTEIN**
- **427 kcal**

Serves 4

1 onion
1 red pepper
2 carrots
4 garlic cloves
7oz (200g) tempeh
3 tbsp chipotle paste
2 tbsp tomato paste
¾oz (20g) nutritional yeast
1 x 14.5oz (411g) can diced tomatoes
1 x 15oz (425g) can black beans
1 cup (200ml) vegetable stock
¼oz (10g) 70% plain chocolate
2 tsp maple (or agave) syrup
2 tsp liquid smoke (optional)
freshly ground black pepper

For the charred eggplants
2 large eggplants
2 tsp dried oregano
1 tbsp ground cumin
1 tbsp sweet smoked paprika
2 tsp ground cilantro
1 tsp ground cinnamon
1 tsp chipotle chili flakes (optional)
4 tbsp olive oil
generous pinch of sea salt, plus extra to season

To serve
long-grain brown rice
tortilla chips
Fresh Green Drizzle (see p216)

Smoky, spicy, and satisfying. A combination of grilled eggplant, crumbled tempeh, and warming spices are simmered in a rich chipotle tomato sauce and finished with a touch of plain chocolate and maple syrup for all-around depth and balance. Great flavor, easy to batch, and even better the next day. Enjoy!

Before you start: you will need a large, deep skillet (or pot). Preheat the grill to high.

Prep eggplants. Slice each eggplant into quarters lengthwise, then cut into ½in (1cm) wide strips. Mix the oregano and ground spices with 2 tablespoons of the olive oil in a large bowl and season with a generous pinch of salt. Add the eggplants and turn until coated. Cook the eggplants under the preheated grill for 10–15 minutes (checking frequently), turning once or twice until charred in places. It's fine if the eggplant blackens as it provides great flavor.

Prep chili. Meanwhile, finely chop the onion and red pepper, discarding the seedy core, then grate the carrots. Peel and grate the garlic. Crumble the tempeh into small ½in (1cm) chunks.

Cook chili. Heat the remaining 2 tablespoons of olive oil in a large, deep skillet over medium–high heat. Add the onion, pepper, and carrots and a little salt and cook for 6–7 minutes, until softened. Stir in the garlic, tempeh, chipotle paste, tomato paste, and nutritional yeast, then cook for a couple of minutes, stirring, to combine. Add in the canned tomatoes, black beans (including their liquid), and stock. Season with salt and bring to a simmer. Cook for about 1 hour, adding the grilled eggplant when ready and topping off with water, if needed, until reduced and thickened.

Assemble and serve. Remove the pan from the heat and stir in the chocolate, maple syrup, and liquid smoke, if using. Season with extra salt and pepper, if needed. Divide among bowls and serve with rice and tortilla chips. Top with the green drizzle and tuck in.

Store. If not serving right away, store in the fridge in one large or individual containers for up to 4 days or freeze for up to 3 months.

PROTEIN-PACKED BLACK DAL

PER PORTION:
- **10.25 PLANT POINTS**
- **41g PROTEIN**
- **693 kcal**

Serves about 4

1 onion
3 garlic cloves
thumb-sized piece of fresh ginger
10oz (300g) silken tofu
9oz (250g) urad dal (split black lentils)
2 tbsp coconut oil
1 tbsp cumin seeds
1 tsp chili flakes
1 tbsp garam masala
2 tsp ground cilantro
1 tsp ground turmeric
1 tsp sweet smoked paprika
pinch of sea salt, plus extra to season
1 x 14.5oz (411g) can diced tomatoes
4 cups (1 liter) vegetable stock

For the spicy tofu
10oz (300g) firm tofu
2 tbsp coconut oil
1 tsp ground cumin
1 tsp garam masala
¼ tsp ground turmeric
¼ tsp freshly ground black pepper

For the chili mango yogurt
7oz (200g) coconut yogurt
2½oz (75g) mango chutney
2 tsp chili crisp (solids from crispy chili oil)

To serve
nigella seeds
cilantro leaves
1 lime
plant-based naan (or brown rice)

This rich, comforting dal is made with split black lentils and blended silken tofu for extra protein. Topped with crispy spiced tofu and chili mango yogurt, it's bold, creamy, and perfect for a Friday night.

Before you start: you will need a large saucepan and a large, nonstick skillet.

Prep dal. Peel and finely chop the onion. Peel and grate the garlic and ginger. Whisk the silken tofu until smooth. Rinse the lentils in a sieve under cold running water until the water runs clear, then let drain.

Cook dal. Heat the coconut oil in a large saucepan over medium heat. Add the cumin seeds, chili flakes, and ground spices and cook for 2–3 minutes. Add the onion and a pinch of salt and cook for 6–8 minutes, until softened, then stir in the garlic and ginger. Add the canned tomatoes, lentils, vegetable stock, and silken tofu. Bring up to boiling, then turn the heat down and simmer gently, stirring occasionally, for 40–45 minutes, until the lentils are soft and creamy.

Make spicy tofu. Meanwhile, drain the tofu and pat dry with paper towels to remove any excess moisture. Crumble the tofu into small chunks. Heat the coconut oil in a large skillet over medium-high heat. Add the tofu and a little salt and cook for 8–10 minutes, turning occasionally, until golden and crisp. Add the ground cumin, garam masala, turmeric, and black pepper and cook, turning to coat the tofu in the spices, for another 1–2 minutes, until fragrant.

Make chili mango yogurt. In a small bowl, combine the yogurt, chutney, and chili crisp. Set aside.

Assemble and serve. Spoon the dal into bowls and top with the chili mango yogurt and spicy tofu. Sprinkle over a few nigella seeds and cilantro leaves. Cut the lime into wedges for squeezing over the dal and serve with the naan.

Store. If not serving right away, divide the dal into portions and let cool. Store in the fridge for up to 4 days or freeze for up to 3 months.

BARBACOA MUSHROOM BEANS

PER PORTION:
- **10.25 PLANT POINTS**
- **12g PROTEIN**
- **170 kcal**

Serves 8

1 large onion
4 garlic cloves
2¼lb (1kg) portobello mushrooms
2 tbsp olive oil
pinch of sea salt, plus extra to season
2 tsp ground cumin
2 tsp sweet smoked paprika
2 tsp dried oregano
1 tbsp tomato paste
2 tbsp chipotle paste
1 tbsp apple cider vinegar
2 x 15oz (425g) cans black beans
1 x 15oz (439g) can pinto (or kidney) beans
1 x 14.5oz (411g) can diced tomatoes
1¾ cups (400ml) vegetable stock
2 limes
freshly ground black pepper

To serve
red chile
1 lime
cilantro leaves
nutritional yeast
tortillas, preferably whole wheat (or brown rice)

Inspired by the classic Mexican barbacoa, this version swaps the slowly braised, spiced meat for mushrooms and beans. They are slow-cooked with chipotle, lime, and cumin. It's smoky, hearty, and perfect with rice or warm tortillas for scooping.

Before you start: you will need a large, deep skillet with lid (or casserole).

Prep vegetables. Finely chop the onion and peel and mince the garlic. Clean and slice the mushrooms.

Cook base. Heat the olive oil in a large, deep skillet over medium heat. Add the onion and a pinch of salt and cook for 6–8 minutes, until soft and golden. Add the garlic, ground cumin, smoked paprika, and oregano, and cook for another minute, stirring, until fragrant. Stir in the tomato paste and chipotle paste, cook for another minute, then pour in the vinegar and stir to deglaze the pan.

Add mushrooms and beans. Drain and rinse all the canned beans. Add in the mushrooms and cook for 8–10 minutes, until any liquid has evaporated and they have taken on a little color. Add the canned beans, canned tomatoes, and vegetable stock, stir well and bring to a simmer. Turn the heat down slightly, part-cover with a lid, and simmer gently for 25 minutes, until rich and thickened. Squeeze the juice of 2 limes and stir two-thirds of the juice into the pan, or to taste. Season with salt and pepper and extra lime juice, if you like—it should taste fresh and limey.

Assemble and serve. Slice the chile and cut the lime into wedges. Ladle the barbacoa into bowls and garnish with cilantro leaves, a sprinkling of nutritional yeast, and the chiles. Serve with warm tortillas and wedges of lime for squeezing over.

Store. If not serving right away, divide the barbacoa into portions and let cool. Store in the fridge for up to 4 days or freeze for up to 3 months.

BAKED APRICOT DAL

PER PORTION:
- **8.5 PLANT POINTS**
- **22g PROTEIN**
- **477 kcal**

Serves 4

1 onion
2 red onions
3 garlic cloves
2 in (5 cm) piece of fresh ginger
2½oz (75g) dried apricots, plus extra to serve
3 tbsp neutral oil of your choice
2 tbsp tamarind paste
1 tbsp cumin seeds
1 tbsp mild curry powder
1 tbsp garam masala
1 tsp ground turmeric
½ tsp chili powder
generous pinch of sea salt, plus extra to season
9oz (250g) split red lentils
3 tbsp apricot jam
1 x 14.5oz (411g) can diced tomatoes
1 x 13.5oz (400ml) can coconut milk
3 cups (750ml) vegetable stock
¾oz (20g) nutritional yeast

To serve
green chiles
cilantro leaves
brown basmati rice (or plant-based naan)

The perfect balance of spicy, savory, and sweet. The dal is great on its own, with rice, or paired with a crunchy, zippy salad.

Before you start: you will need a large, shallow casserole (or large, deep, ovenproof skillet). Preheat your oven to 400°F (200°C).

Prep ingredients. Finely chop the onion. Slice the red onions into ¼ in (5 mm) thick rounds. Peel and grate the garlic and ginger. Finely chop the dried apricots. Whisk 1 tablespoon of the oil into the tamarind paste in a small bowl, then set aside.

Start dal. Heat the remaining 2 tablespoons of oil in a large, shallow casserole over medium heat. Add the cumin seeds, curry powder, garam masala, turmeric, and chili powder and cook for about 20–30 seconds, until foaming and fragrant. Add the chopped onion and a generous pinch of salt and cook for 7–8 minutes, until soft and beginning to caramelize, adding a little water if the onion starts to catch. Add the garlic and ginger and cook for a minute or two until fragrant.

Add lentils. Rinse the lentils in a sieve under cold running water until the water runs clear, then drain well. Add the lentils, apricot jam, chopped apricots, canned tomatoes, coconut milk, stock, and nutritional yeast. Season with salt, then stir until combined. Bring to a gentle simmer, then reduce the heat to low and heat through briefly.

Bake. Top the lentil mixture with an even layer of the sliced red onions, then spoon over the tamarind mixture to glaze. Season with salt and bake in the oven for 40 minutes, until the lentils are tender and the onions are caramelized and jammy. (For extra-caramelized onions, finish cooking the dish under the grill for about 5 minutes.)

Serve. Carefully remove the dish from the oven (or grill). Chop some extra dried apricots and sprinkle them over the top with a few sliced green chiles and cilantro leaves. Serve with basmati rice on the side.

Store. Let the dal cool and store in the fridge for up to 3 days or freeze for up to 3 months.

GALWAY STEW

PER PORTION:
- **11 PLANT POINTS**
- **17g PROTEIN**
- **409 kcal**

Serves 8

2 onions
3 carrots
3 celery stalks
2 parsnips
2¼lb(1kg) brown button mushrooms
2¾lb (1.2kg) small Yukon Golds (or other baby new potatoes)
4 tbsp olive oil
generous pinch of salt, plus extra to season
⅓ cup (100ml) water
2 tbsp tomato paste
2 cups (500ml) Guinness (or other vegan-friendly Irish stout)
3½oz (100g) pearl barley (or split red lentils)
2 tbsp yeast extract (such as brewer's yeast or Marmite)
2 tbsp light soy sauce
1 tbsp white or brown miso
2 × 15.5oz (439g) cans borlotti beans
5½ cups (1.3 liters) vegetable stock
freshly ground black pepper

For the bouquet garni
6 thyme sprigs
2 rosemary sprigs
2 bay leaves

To serve
parsley leaves
crusty whole wheat bread (or soda bread)

Traditional Irish stew usually relies on lamb for depth. Ours uses meaty mushrooms, stout, and Marmite for richness, with chunky vegetables and barley for something hearty, wholesome, and full of flavor. Roll on winter!

Before you start: you will need kitchen string and a large, heavy-based casserole (or saucepan with lid).

Prep vegetables. Peel and thinly slice the onions. Roughly chop the carrots, celery, parsnips, and mushrooms into small 1 in (2.5 cm) chunks. Halve any large potatoes.

Make bouquet garni. Tie the thyme, rosemary, and bay leaves together with kitchen string to make a bouquet garni. Set aside.

Make stew base. Heat the olive oil in a large casserole over medium heat. Add the onions with a generous pinch of salt and then add the water, cover, and cook for about 15 minutes, stirring occasionally, until translucent. Remove the lid, increase the heat to medium-high and cook for a further 5–10 minutes, stirring regularly, until golden and caramelized. Add the carrots, celery, parsnips, and mushrooms, and cook for 7–8 minutes, until the mushrooms have released their liquid and the vegetables are lightly golden. Stir in the tomato paste and cook for 2 minutes.

Deglaze and cook stew. Pour in the Guinness and stir well, scraping up any stuck bits from the bottom of the casserole. Add the barley, yeast extract, soy sauce, and miso. Bring up to boiling, then turn the heat down slightly and simmer for 10 minutes, or until the Guinness has reduced by half. Drain and add the borlotti beans to the casserole with the potatoes, stock, and bouquet garni. Bring to a simmer, cover with the lid, and cook for 35–40 minutes, until the barley is tender and the potatoes are cooked through.

Assemble and serve. Remove the bouquet garni and season to taste with salt and pepper. Sprinkle over the parsley and serve with slices of crusty bread.

Store. If not serving right away, divide the stew into portions and let cool. Store in the fridge for up to 4 days or freeze for up to 3 months.

WALNUT MINCE RAPID RAGÙ

PER PORTION:

- 6 PLANT POINTS
- 18g PROTEIN
- 501 kcal

Serves 4

1¾ cup (200g) walnut pieces
1lb 8oz (700g) brown button mushrooms
3 garlic cloves
2 tbsp olive oil
1 tbsp tomato paste
2 x 14.5oz (411g) cans diced tomatoes
pinch of sugar
1 tsp bouillon powder
2 tbsp brewer's yeast or Marmite
sea salt and freshly ground black pepper

To serve
gnocchi (or whole wheat pasta shape of your choice)
plant-based parmesan or nutritional yeast

A speedy, go-to ragù that's rich, savory, and utterly satisfying. Crumbled walnuts and mushrooms create a meaty texture that pairs perfectly with your favorite carb. What's more, by switching up just a few ingredients, you can turn this ragù into a Bolognese, chili, or fragrant tagine (see the recipes on p144–145). It makes a great base for variety any day of the week!

Before you start: you will need a food processor and a large skillet (or saucepan).

Prep ingredients. Finely chop or roughly grind/pulse the walnuts in a food processor into small pieces. Roughly chop the mushrooms or coarsely grate with a cheese grater. Peel and grate the garlic.

Make ragù base. Heat the olive oil in a large skillet. Add the mushrooms and cook for 6–7 minutes, until softened and any moisture has evaporated. Stir in the garlic and tomato paste and cook for 2–3 minutes, stirring occasionally, until fragrant. Add the walnuts and the canned tomatoes, a pinch of sugar, the bouillon powder, and brewer's yeast.

Cook ragù. Bring the sauce up to a simmer and cook for 10–15 minutes, stirring occasionally, until reduced and thickened. Season to taste with salt and pepper.

Assemble and serve. Spoon the ragù over the gnocchi and finish with a sprinkling of plant-based parmesan or nutritional yeast.

Store. If not serving right away, divide the ragù into portions and let cool. Store in the fridge for up to 5 days or freeze for up to 3 months.

BOLOGNESE

PER PORTION:
- **9 PLANT POINTS**
- **19g PROTEIN**
- **413 kcal**

Serves 6

1 recipe quantity of the Walnut Mince Rapid Ragù (see p164)
9oz (250g) cooked lentils, beluga or puy work well
⅔ cup (10g) basil leaves, plus extra to serve
1 bay leaf
2 tbsp nutritional yeast
sea salt and freshly ground black pepper

To serve
whole wheat spaghetti
plant-based parmesan

Prep walnut ragù. Follow the instructions for making the Walnut Mince Rapid Ragù (see p164) up to the "Cook ragù" step.

Add Bolognese ingredients. Before cooking the ragù, stir in the lentils, basil leaves, and bay leaf, and simmer for 10–15 minutes, topping off with a little water, if needed, until reduced and thickened. Remove the bay leaf and stir in the nutritional yeast. Taste and season with salt and pepper.

Assemble and serve. Spoon the sauce over spaghetti to serve, and finish with a sprinkling of plant-based parmesan and extra basil leaves.

Store. If not serving right away, divide the Bolognese into portions and let cool. Store in the fridge for up to 5 days or freeze for up to 3 months.

CHILI

PER PORTION:
- **10.5 PLANT POINTS**
- **15g PROTEIN**
- **390 kcal**

Serves 6

1 recipe quantity of the Walnut Mince Rapid Ragù (see p164)
2 tsp hot chili powder
2 tsp ground cumin
2 tsp paprika
1 tsp dried marjoram
1 x 15.5oz (400g) can kidney beans
⅔ cup (10g) cilantro leaves, plus extra to serve
sea salt and freshly ground black pepper

To serve
long-grain brown rice
plant-based sour cream
guacamole

Prep walnut ragù. Follow the instructions for making the Walnut Mince Rapid Ragù (see p164) up to the "Cook ragù" step.

Add chili ingredients. Before cooking the ragù, add the chili powder, ground cumin, paprika, and marjoram. Drain the kidney beans, then stir them into the sauce and simmer for 10–15 minutes, topping off with a little water, if needed, until reduced and thickened. Remove from the heat and stir through the cilantro leaves. Taste and season with salt and pepper.

Assemble and serve. Serve the chili with rice and topped with plant-based sour cream, guacamole, and extra cilantro leaves.

Store. If not serving right away, divide the chili into portions and let cool. Store in the fridge for up to 5 days or freeze for up to 3 months.

TAGINE

PER PORTION:

- 10.75 PLANT POINTS
- 15g PROTEIN
- 410 kcal

Serves 6

1 recipe quantity of the Walnut Mince Rapid Ragù (see p164)
2 tsp ground cumin
2 tsp ground cilantro
1 tsp ground all-spice
1 tsp hot chili powder
½ tsp ground turmeric
⅓ cup (75g) raisins
1 x 15oz (425g) can chickpeas
⅔ cup (10g) parsley leaves, plus extra to serve
sea salt and freshly ground black pepper

To serve
whole wheat couscous

Prep walnut ragù. Follow the instructions for making the Walnut Mince Rapid Ragù (see p164) up to the "Cook ragù" step.

Add tagine ingredients. Before cooking the ragù, stir in the ground cumin, cilantro, all-spice, chili powder, turmeric, and raisins. Drain the chickpeas, then stir them into the sauce and simmer for 10–15 minutes, topping off with a little water, if needed, until reduced and thickened. Turn off the heat, finely chop the parsley leaves, then stir through the tagine. Taste and season with salt and pepper.

Assemble and serve. Serve the tagine with couscous, sprinkled with extra parsley leaves.

Store. If not serving right away, divide the tagine into portions and let cool. Store in the fridge for up to 5 days or freeze for up to 3 months.

CREAMY NOOCH & BROCCOLI SOUP
(WITH BROCCOLI SALSA)

PER PORTION:
- 10 PLANT POINTS
- 15g PROTEIN
- 344 kcal

Serves 6

1 large head of broccoli
2 medium onions
2 medium leeks
2 medium potatoes
4 garlic cloves
3 tbsp olive oil
1¾oz (50g) nooch (aka nutritional yeast)
⅓ cup (50g) raw cashew nuts
7 cups (1.75 liters) vegetable stock
2½ cups (80g) spinach leaves
½ lemon
sea salt and freshly ground black pepper

For the broccoli salsa

2 tbsp red wine vinegar
2 tbsp extra-virgin olive oil
3 tbsp Brain Power seed blend (see p209), or 3 tbsp mixed seeds of choice

A creamy, comforting broccoli soup boosted with nutritional yeast and cashews. It's finished with a tangy, crunchy, charred broccoli salsa for texture and extra plant-rich goodness.

Before you start: you will need a large saucepan with lid and an immersion blender (or high-speed blender). Line a large baking sheet with parchment paper. Preheat the oven to 425°F (220°C).

Prep ingredients. Cut the broccoli into florets and the stalk into 1 in (2.5 cm) chunks. Finely slice the onions and leeks. Cut the potatoes into 1 in (2.5 cm) cubes (no need to peel) and set aside.

Make soup base. Add the broccoli to one side of the lined baking sheet and the onions and leeks to the other, ensuring they are separate. Add the whole garlic cloves, slotting them between the vegetables. Drizzle over the olive oil and add ¼oz (10g) of the nutritional yeast. Season with salt and pepper. Roast in the preheated oven for 20–25 minutes, until the vegetables are tender, and the broccoli is slightly charred at the edges. Pour the roasted vegetables into a large saucepan, reserving about one-third of the broccoli, setting it aside.

Simmer soup. Squeeze the garlic out of its skin into the pan. Add the potatoes, cashews, and stock. Bring up to a simmer and cook for 15 minutes, until the potatoes are tender. Add the spinach and the remaining 1½oz (40g) of nutritional yeast and remove from the heat.

Blend soup. Using an electric hand blender, carefully blend the soup until smooth and creamy (or transfer the soup to a blender and blend in batches). Squeeze in the juice of ½ lemon. Taste and season with salt and pepper. Put the lid on while you make the salsa.

Make salsa. Finely chop the reserved roasted broccoli and mix with the vinegar, extra-virgin olive oil, and the seeds in a bowl.

Assemble and serve. Ladle the soup into bowls. Spoon over the broccoli salsa and serve.

Store. If not serving right away, store in an airtight container in the fridge for up to 3 days or freeze (soup only) for up to 3 months.

MORE PLANTS SIGNATURE SAUCE

PER PORTION:

- 8 PLANT POINTS
- 8g PROTEIN
- 206 kcal

Serves 4

2 onions
2 carrots
2 celery stalks
4 garlic cloves
4 large, ripe tomatoes
1 x 28oz (793g) cans peeled San Marzano tomatoes (or good-quality plum tomatoes)
4 basil sprigs
2 rosemary sprigs
5 thyme sprigs
1 bay leaf
2 tbsp extra-virgin olive oil
generous pinch of sea salt, plus extra to season
2 tbsp tomato paste
2 cups (500ml) fresh vegetable stock
2–3 Green Plant Point Cubes (see p215), or 1 large handful of spinach leaves
½oz (15g) nutritional yeast
pinch of sugar
freshly ground black pepper
your choice of pasta, to serve

This is your new go-to pasta sauce. Simmer it low and slow for rich depth, as here, or you could speed things up by making the stock with a cube or pot and reducing the amount to ⅔ cup/150ml. Simply add the stock with the rest of the ingredients and cook the sauce for 20 minutes on the stove. Now, pass the pasta!

Before you start: you will need kitchen string and a large saucepan.

Prep ingredients. Finely chop the onions, carrots, and celery (or coarsely grate with a cheese grater). Peel and mince the garlic. Roughly chop the fresh tomatoes. Pour the canned tomatoes into a large bowl and squeeze thoroughly by hand to break up into small pieces. (This is a tip we learned from one of the world's great pizza chefs, Michele from the restaurant *Napoli on the Road*.)

Make bouquet garni. Cut a 6 in (15 cm) length of kitchen string and place it on your work surface. Lay the basil, rosemary, thyme, and bay leaf on the string. Twist the string around the stalks of the herbs a few times to make an herb bundle, then secure with a knot. Set aside.

Make sauce. Heat the olive oil in a large pan over medium heat. Add the onions, carrots, and celery and a generous pinch of salt and cook for 10–15 minutes, stirring occasionally, until the vegetables are very soft and starting to take on a little color. Stir in the garlic and cook for 1–2 minutes, until fragrant, then add the tomato paste and fresh chopped tomatoes, stir for another few minutes. Add in the squeezed canned tomatoes, stock, and herb bundle, and bring up to boiling. Reduce the heat to a gentle simmer and cook for at least 1 hour, stirring occasionally to prevent the sauce from sticking to the base of the pan, until reduced and thickened. If the sauce becomes dry, top off with a splash of water.

Finish sauce. Remove the bouquet garni and add the green cubes and nutritional yeast, then stir for a few minutes until defrosted and heated through. Taste and adjust the seasoning with salt, pepper, and a pinch of sugar, if needed. Serve the sauce tossed with your favorite pasta shape—it also works as a great sauce on pizza.

Store. If not serving right away, store in the fridge in one large or individual containers for up to 1 week or freeze for up to 3 months.

MASSAMAN LIMA BEANS

PER PORTION:
- 12.25 PLANT POINTS
- 9g PROTEIN
- 400 kcal

Serves about 6

1 onion
14oz (400g) baby or new potatoes
2 carrots
1 red pepper
2 tbsp coconut (or neutral) oil
2 x 15.5oz (439g) cans lima beans
1 x 13.5 oz (400ml) can coconut cream
1½ cups (350ml) vegetable stock
2 tsp light soy sauce
1 tbsp maple syrup (or coconut sugar)
1 lime

For the massaman paste (or use store-bought)

2 small shallots
4 garlic cloves
2 in (5 cm) piece of galangal
1–2 mild red chiles
1 lemongrass stalk
1 tsp cilantro seeds
1 tsp cumin seeds
2 cardamom pods
½ tsp ground cinnamon
½ tsp freshly ground black or white pepper
1 tsp coconut sugar or brown sugar
pinch of salt, plus extra to season
2 tbsp neutral oil of your choice

To serve

brown jasmine rice
roasted unsalted peanuts
cilantro leaves
1 lime

A rich, fragrant Thai-inspired curry made with lima beans, baby potatoes, and a creamy coconut massaman sauce. Cozy, comforting, and perfect with jasmine rice, peanuts, and a good squeeze of lime.

Before you start: you will need a small food processor (or pestle and mortar) and a large casserole (or saucepan).

Make paste (if using homemade). Peel and roughly chop the shallots, garlic, and galangal. Roughly chop the chiles. Peel the lemongrass and roughly chop the inner stalk. Add the cilantro, cumin, and cardamom seeds to a small food processor and pulse to a fine powder. Add the ground cinnamon, black pepper, shallots, garlic, galangal, chiles, sugar, salt, and oil, and blend to a thick, smooth paste, scraping down the sides as needed. Add a splash of water, if necessary, to loosen the paste. Set aside.

Prep curry vegetables. Peel and finely dice the onion. Peel and chop the potatoes and carrots into 1 in (2.5 cm) bite-sized pieces. Slice the red pepper, discarding the seedy core.

Make curry. Heat the coconut oil in a large casserole over medium heat. Add the onion and a little salt, and cook for 5–7 minutes, until softened. Stir in 4 tablespoons of the massaman paste and cook, stirring regularly, for 3–4 minutes, until fragrant. Drain the lima beans and add to the casserole with the potatoes and carrots, stirring to coat them in the paste. Add the coconut cream, stock, soy sauce, and maple syrup and bring up to a simmer. Cover with the lid and cook for 25 minutes, adding the red pepper halfway through, until the vegetables are tender and the sauce has thickened slightly. Squeeze in the juice of 1 lime and season with extra salt and pepper, if needed.

Assemble and serve. Serve the curry in bowls with jasmine rice, topped with roughly chopped peanuts and cilantro leaves. Cut the lime into wedges and serve on the side for squeezing.

Store and reheat. Store the spice paste in the fridge for up to 1 week or freeze in portions for up to 1 month. If not serving the massaman curry right away, divide it into portions and let cool. Store in the fridge for up to 3 days or freeze for up to 3 months.

MIGHTY PLANT-BASED CHILI

PER PORTION:

- **15.75 PLANT POINTS**
- **19g PROTEIN**
- **303 kcal**

Serves about 8

For the "ground meat"

9½oz (280g) firm tofu
14oz (400g) brown button mushrooms
7oz (200g) tempeh
3 tbsp olive oil
sea salt and freshly ground black pepper

For the chili

2 red onions
4 garlic cloves
2 red chiles
1¼ cup (20g) cilantro
1 celery stalk
1 red pepper
1 x 15oz (425g) can kidney beans
1 x 15oz (425g) can black beans
1 tbsp olive oil
1 tsp hot chili powder
1 tsp ground cumin
1 tsp hot smoked paprika
½ tsp ground cinnamon
½ tsp dried oregano
1 bay leaf
1 tbsp tomato paste
1 cup (250ml) red wine
1 tsp balsamic vinegar
2 tsp light soy sauce
2 x 14.5oz (411g) cans diced tomatoes
1 cup (200ml) vegetable stock
1½ tsp maple (or agave) syrup
¼oz (10g) 70% plain chocolate

To serve

long-grain brown rice and/or tortilla chips
guacamole and/or salsa

"Where do you get your protein from?" Here. We get our protein from the tofu, tempeh, and beans in this dish, and now you can, too. Hearty, satisfying, and packed with flavor. Enjoy!

Before you start: you will need a large casserole (or saucepan).

Make "ground meat." Drain the tofu and pat dry with paper towels to remove any excess moisture. Grate the mushrooms, tofu, and tempeh with a cheese grater. Heat the olive oil in a large saucepan over medium heat. Add the mushrooms, tofu, and tempeh, season, and cook for 10–12 minutes, until golden. Spoon into a bowl.

Prep chili. Peel and dice the onions. Peel and grate the garlic. Halve, seed, and dice the chiles. Pick the cilantro leaves and finely slice half of the stalks. Finely slice the celery and dice the red pepper, discarding the seedy core. Drain the canned beans.

Start chili. Heat the olive oil in the same large saucepan over medium heat. Add the onions and a little salt and cook for 2–3 minutes, then add the celery and red pepper and cook for a further 4–5 minutes. Add the garlic, chiles, and cilantro stalks (save the leaves for later), and cook for 2 minutes, stirring, until fragrant. Add the ground spices, oregano, and bay leaf, and cook for 2 minutes, stirring. Add the tomato paste and stir for another minute. Pour in the red wine, vinegar, and soy sauce, and simmer for 6–7 minutes, until reduced by half, stirring occasionally to prevent it from catching on the bottom of the pan.

Finish chili. Add the canned tomatoes and stock. Bring to a simmer and cook for 5–6 minutes, stirring occasionally. Add the canned beans, maple syrup, and the cooked "ground meat" and simmer for 15 minutes, stirring occasionally. Stir in the cilantro leaves and chocolate until melted. Taste and season with salt and pepper.

Assemble and serve. Bring the chili to the table and serve with rice and/or tortilla chips and guacamole and/or salsa.

Store. If not serving right away, divide the chili into portions and let cool. Store in the fridge for up to 5 days or freeze for up to 3 months.

TOFU TIKKA MASALA

PER PORTION:

- 11.5 PLANT POINTS
- 39g PROTEIN
- 641 kcal

Serves about 6

For the tofu tikka
1lb 8oz (700g) extra-firm tofu
5 garlic cloves
2 in (5 cm) piece of fresh ginger
1 red chile
1 bunch of cilantro
9oz (250g) coconut (or plant-based) unsweetened yogurt
1 tbsp ground cumin
1 tbsp garam masala
1 tbsp ground cilantro
1 tsp ground turmeric
1 tsp ground nutmeg (optional)
sea salt and freshly ground black pepper

For the curry
2 onions
1lb 5oz (600g) brown button mushrooms
1 small cauliflower
25oz (700g) cooked chickpeas
3 tbsp neutral oil of your choice
1 tbsp mustard seeds
1 tbsp ground cumin
1 tbsp garam masala
1 tbsp mild or hot curry powder
2 x 14.5oz (411g) cans diced tomatoes
1 x 13.5 oz (400ml) can coconut milk
1 vegetable stock pot
4 tbsp nutritional yeast
maple (or agave) syrup (optional)

To serve
brown rice (or plant-based naan)
Fresh Green Drizzle (see p216)

Tikka masala is a British classic, often dubbed the nation's favorite dish. Our version keeps the familiar rich creaminess, but it's also brimming with plant-rich protein from the tofu and chickpeas.

Before you start: you will need a large, deep skillet (or wok). Line a large baking sheet with parchment paper. Preheat the oven to 475°F (240°C).

Prep tofu. Drain the tofu and pat dry with paper towels to remove any excess moisture. Tear the tofu into bite-sized chunks. Peel and grate the garlic and ginger. Finely chop the chile, removing the seeds. Finely slice the cilantro stalks (use the leaves in the drizzle). Spoon the yogurt into a large bowl with the ground spices, ginger, chile, cilantro stalks, and half of the garlic. Season, add the tofu pieces, and give everything a good mix so the chunks are coated.

Cook tofu. Transfer the tofu to a lined baking sheet, and cook in the oven for 40 minutes, turning halfway, until deep golden.

Prep ingredients for curry. Meanwhile, peel and finely chop the onions. Roughly chop or grate the mushrooms. Cut the cauliflower into small 1 in (2.5 cm) chunks. Drain and rinse the chickpeas.

Make curry. Heat the oil in a large, deep skillet over medium heat. Add the mustard seeds and cook until they start to pop, then stir in the ground spices and cook for another 30 seconds. Add the onions and mushrooms and cook for 7–8 minutes, until tender. Add the remaining garlic and cook for a minute or two. Add in the canned tomatoes, coconut milk, and stock pot. Add the chickpeas and season with salt and pepper. Turn the heat down slightly and simmer for 10–15 minutes, stirring occasionally, until thickened. Stir the cauliflower into the pan and cook for a further 5 minutes, until just tender. Stir in the roasted tofu and nutritional yeast, taste and season with salt, pepper, and a little maple syrup, if you like.

Assemble and serve. Spoon the tofu tikka onto plates and serve with rice and a spoonful of the green drizzle.

Store. If not serving right away, divide the curry into portions and let cool. Store in the fridge for up to 4 days or freeze for up to 3 months.

SWEET ROAST TOMATO & CHILI SOUP

PER PORTION:

- **6.25 PLANT POINTS**
- **18g PROTEIN**
- **349 kcal**

Serves about 4

4 shallots
2¼lb (1kg) ripe tomatoes of choice
2 Romano peppers
1–2 red chiles, depending on heat
1 whole garlic bulb
6 thyme sprigs
2 tbsp extra-virgin olive oil
2 cups (500ml) vegetable stock
1 tbsp balsamic vinegar
2 tsp maple (or agave) syrup
1 cup (200ml) plant-based cream, plus extra for drizzling
sea salt and freshly ground black pepper

For the crispy maple chickpeas
1 x 15oz (425g) can chickpeas
1 tbsp olive oil
1 tbsp maple (or agave) syrup

To serve
chili oil
crusty sourdough (or focaccia)

Roasting the tomatoes, peppers, and garlic brings out a deep, sweet flavor with a smoky edge. Blended until silky smooth and topped with crispy maple chickpeas, this is soup at its best.

Before you start: you will need a large saucepan and an immersion blender (or high-speed blender). Line 2 large baking sheets with parchment paper. Preheat the oven to 475°F (240°C).

Prep vegetables. Peel and slice the shallots in half lengthwise. Cut the tomatoes into even-sized chunks. Roughly chop the peppers, discarding the seeds. Seed the chiles, if preferred. Cut the garlic bulb in half through the middle.

Roast vegetables. Place the shallots, tomatoes, peppers, chiles, garlic, and thyme on one of the lined baking sheets. Drizzle over the olive oil and season with salt and pepper, then toss to combine. Roast for 30–35 minutes, turning halfway, until softened and slightly charred.

Make crispy maple chickpeas. Meanwhile, drain and rinse the chickpeas and put them onto the second lined baking sheet. Drizzle over the olive oil and maple syrup, then season. Roast for 13–17 minutes, stirring halfway, until crisp. Let cool and crisp up further.

Cook and blend soup. Remove the thyme sprigs, squeeze the garlic cloves into a large saucepan, then add the roasted vegetables, chiles, stock, vinegar, and maple syrup. Bring up to a simmer and cook for 10–15 minutes. Stir in the plant-based cream, then blend the soup with an immersion blender (or transfer to a blender in batches) and blend until smooth and creamy. Taste, reheating the soup, if needed, and season with salt and pepper.

Assemble and serve. Ladle the soup into bowls, top with the crispy chickpeas, an extra drizzle of plant-based cream, and the chili oil. Finish with a good grinding of pepper. Serve with crusty sourdough or focaccia.

Store. If not serving right away, divide the soup into portions and let cool. Store in the fridge for up to 4 days or freeze for up to 3 months. Keep the crispy chickpeas in an airtight container for up to 2 days.

EGGPLANT, APRICOT & OLIVE TAGINE

PER PORTION:
- 11.75 PLANT POINTS
- 8.5g PROTEIN
- 266 kcal

Serves 6

1 large onion
2 carrots
2 eggplants
5 garlic cloves
2 in (5 cm) piece of fresh ginger
1 x 15oz (425g) can chickpeas
2 tbsp olive oil
generous pinch of salt, plus extra to season
½ tbsp ground cumin
½ tbsp ground cilantro
1 tbsp sweet smoked paprika
½ tsp ground cinnamon
½ tsp cayenne pepper (optional heat)
2 tbsp tomato paste
1 x 14.5oz (411g) can diced tomatoes
2½ cups (600ml) vegetable stock
5½oz (150g) dried apricots
5½oz (150g) pitted mixed olives
½oz (15g) nutritional yeast
1 tbsp lemon juice
freshly ground black pepper

To serve

toasted pine nuts (or sliced almonds)
cilantro and/or parsley
couscous, quinoa, or crusty bread, preferably whole wheat (optional)

A rich, gently spiced tagine with tender eggplant, sweet apricots, and salty olives. Slow cooked until thick and flavorful, it's perfect with couscous or warm bread to mop up the sauce.

Before you start: you will need a large casserole or saucepan.

Prep ingredients. Peel and dice the onion. Cut the carrots and eggplants into bite-sized chunks. Peel and grate the garlic and ginger. Drain the chickpeas.

Cook tagine base. Heat the oil in a large saucepan over medium heat. Add the onion and carrots and cook for around 3 minutes, until beginning to soften. Add the eggplants with a generous pinch of salt and cook, stirring occasionally, for another 5–6 minutes, until the vegetables begin to turn golden. Add the ginger and garlic and cook for another minute until fragrant, then stir in the ground cumin, ground cilantro, smoked paprika, cinnamon, and cayenne pepper, if using, and cook for 1 minute, until fragrant. Add the tomato paste and cook for 30 seconds, stirring.

Simmer tagine. Add the canned tomatoes, vegetables stock, dried apricots, olives, nutritional yeast, and chickpeas and stir until combined, scraping up any spices from the bottom of the pan, if needed. Bring the tagine up to a boil, then turn the heat down to low and simmer gently for about 25 minutes, stirring occasionally to prevent sticking, until the vegetables are very tender and the tagine has reduced and thickened.

Finish tagine. Remove the pan from the heat and add the lemon juice. Taste and season with salt and pepper.

Assemble and serve. Spoon the tagine into bowls and finish with a sprinkling of pine nuts for crunch and a generous amount of freshly chopped cilantro and/or parsley. This dish is delicious on its own, but you can also serve it with couscous, quinoa, or crusty bread on the side to soak up the rich, spicy sauce.

Store. Let the tagine cool and store in the fridge for up to 4 days or freeze for up to 3 months.

SWEET TREAT

S

CHOCO COCO NUGGETS

PER PORTION:

- 2 PLANT POINTS
- 1g PROTEIN
- 140 kcal

Makes about 20

2½ cups (200g) unsweetened shredded coconut
generous pinch of sea salt
⅓ cup (100ml) coconut milk
2 tbsp coconut oil
2 tbsp maple (or agave) syrup
1 tsp vanilla extract or paste
7oz (200g) 70% plain chocolate

A homemade twist on the classic treat, these chewy, coconutty bites are dipped in rich plain chocolate and chilled until firm. They're sweet, satisfying, and perfect straight from the fridge.

Before you start: you will need a small skillet and a small saucepan. Line a large baking sheet with parchment paper.

Prep shredded coconut. Heat a small, dry skillet over medium heat until hot. Add half of the shredded coconut and toast for 2–3 minutes, until golden. Pour the toasted coconut into a large bowl and mix with the untoasted, then transfer 2 tablespoons of the coconut to a small bowl and set aside. Stir a generous pinch of salt into the coconut in the large bowl.

Prep rest of filling. Add the coconut milk, coconut oil, maple syrup, and vanilla to a small saucepan over low heat and stir until melted. Pour the warm coconut milk mixture into the large bowl containing the toasted and untoasted shredded coconut and stir with a wooden spoon until combined. Leave until cool enough to handle.

Shape nuggets. Form the coconut mixture into about 20 large, bite-sized nuggets and place on the lined baking sheet. Chill in the fridge for 45 minutes to firm up (or you can freeze them for 20 minutes).

Coat with chocolate. Break the chocolate into even-sized chunks, then place in a microwave-safe bowl and microwave in 20-second intervals, stirring each time, until melted and smooth. Working one at a time, use a spoon to dip the chilled coconut nuggets into the melted chocolate until evenly coated. Place the coated nuggets back onto the lined tray. When all the nuggets have been coated, sprinkle over the reserved 2 tablespoons of shredded coconut. Chill the nuggets until the chocolate sets.

Serve and store. When ready, enjoy right away or store in the fridge in an airtight container for up to 10 days. The nuggets can also be frozen for up to 3 months, stored in a freezer-safe container.

MAPLE PECAN BARS

PER PORTION:
- 6 PLANT POINTS
- 5g PROTEIN
- 368 kcal

Makes 12

⅔ cup (150g) coconut oil
⅓ cup (75g) almond butter (or peanut butter)
⅔ cup(150ml) maple (or agave) syrup
1 cup (100g) pecans
2 bananas
2½ cups (250g) old-fashioned rolled oats
⅓ cup (50g) raisins (or golden raisins or currants)
2 tbsp chia seeds
1 tsp vanilla extract or paste
pinch of sea salt

These soft, chewy bars are naturally sweetened, loaded with fiber, and packed with pecans, bananas, and oats. A great snack for lunch boxes, commutes, or after-school pick-me-ups.

Before you start: you will need a small saucepan. Line an 8in (20cm) square baking pan with parchment paper, leaving a slight overhang. Preheat the oven to 350°F (180°C).

Prep wet ingredients. Heat the coconut oil, almond butter, and maple syrup in a small saucepan over low heat, stirring, until melted and combined. Set aside briefly.

Combine mixture. Roughly chop the pecans, and peel and mash the bananas with the back of a fork. Put the pecans and bananas into a large bowl and add the oats, raisins, chia seeds, vanilla, and salt. Pour the warm maple-oil mixture into the bowl and stir well with a wooden spoon until everything is evenly combined. Pour the mixture into the lined baking pan and press down very firmly and evenly, using the back of the spoon.

Bake and portion. Bake for 18–20 minutes, until firm and lightly golden around the edges. While still warm, lightly score the mixutre into 12 bars (4 x 3 grid). Leave in the pan to cool completely, then lift out using the overhanging parchment paper to help you. Portion into bars, using the scored lines as a guide.

Serve and store. Enjoy right away or store in an airtight container in the fridge for up to 10 days. The bars can also be frozen for up to 3 months, stored in a freezer-safe container.

TAHINI & MACADAMIA OAT BISCUITS

PER PORTION:
- **5.25 PLANT POINTS**
- **5g PROTEIN**
- **240 kcal**

Makes 12

1 tbsp ground flaxseeds
⅓ cup(50g) raw macadamia nuts
¼ cup(50g) coconut oil
½ cup (120g) tahini
¼ cup (50ml) plant-based milk
1 tsp vanilla extract
¾ cup (100g) whole wheat flour
1 cup(80g) old-fashioned rolled oats
1 tsp baking powder
⅓ cup(50g) raisins
½ cup (100g) coconut sugar
½ tsp ground cinnamon
¼ tsp sea salt

Crunchy on the outside, soft in the middle, and packed with nutty goodness. Make a batch, load up your cookie jar, and stick the kettle on!

Before you start: you will need a small saucepan. Line a large baking sheet with parchment paper. Preheat the oven to 400°F (200°C).

Prep ingredients. Mix the ground flaxseeds with 3 tablespoons water in a small bowl and set aside for 5 minutes. Finely chop the macadamia nuts.

Prep wet mix. Melt the coconut oil in a small saucepan over low heat. Turn off the heat and stir in the tahini, plant-based milk, vanilla, and flaxseed mixture until combined.

Prep dry mix. Add the macadamia nuts, flour, oats, baking powder, raisins, coconut sugar, cinnamon, and salt to a large mixing bowl and stir to combine.

Shape and bake. Pour the wet mix into the dry mix and stir well with a wooden spoon to combine to a dough. Scoop 12 portions onto the lined baking sheet (around 1½–2 tablespoons of dough per cookie) and flatten the top of each one slightly into a round. Bake in the preheated oven for 12 minutes, until golden and slightly crisp.

Serve and store. Leave on the tray to cool completely and firm up. Store in an airtight jar for up to 5 days—if they last that long.

SILKY CHOC POTS

PER PORTION:

- 5.25 PLANT POINTS
- 7g PROTEIN
- 156 kcal

Makes 8

1¾oz (50g) pitted dried dates
4½oz (120g) 70% plain chocolate
10oz (300g) silken tofu
1 tbsp maple (or agave) syrup
2 tbsp plant-based milk
pinch of sea salt flakes, plus extra to serve (optional)

To serve

fresh fruit of your choice, such as strawberries and cherries
lemon zest

These are delicious ... silky, chocolatey, and luscious. They may just be the perfect make-ahead dessert; simply blend, chill, top, and devour. Enjoy!

Before you start: you will need a high-speed blender.

Prep dates. Roughly chop the dates and put them in a heatproof bowl. Pour over enough just-boiled water from a kettle to cover and leave for 10 minutes, until softened. Drain well and add the dates to a blender.

Melt chocolate. Meanwhile, break the chocolate into even-sized chunks, then place in a microwave-safe bowl and microwave in 20-second intervals, stirring each time, until melted and smooth. Set aside briefly.

Start mousse. Add the silken tofu, maple syrup, plant-based milk, and a pinch of salt to the dates in the blender and blend until creamy and silky smooth. Add the melted chocolate and blend again until combined. Pour the mousse into small serving bowls or glasses and chill for 3 hours, or overnight, to set.

Assemble and serve. When ready to serve, prepare your choice of fruit as needed. Top the chocolate pots with your choice of fresh fruit, lemon zest, and an extra pinch of sea salt flakes, if you like, and enjoy.

Store. If not serving right away, keep up to 2 days in the fridge or freeze for up to 3 months (without the toppings), stored in a freezer-safe container.

MIXED NUT BUTTER– STUFFED DATES

PER DATE:
- 5 PLANT POINTS
- 4g PROTEIN
- 149 kcal

Makes 12 (plus extra nut butter)

1¾oz (50g) 70% plain chocolate
12 Medjool dates

For the nut butter
¾ cup (100g) blanched almonds
¾ cup (100g) raw cashew nuts
¾ cup (100g) unsalted peanuts
1 tbsp sugar (or coconut sugar) (optional)
¼ tsp sea salt, plus extra to taste (optional)

These have been doing the rounds online, so we gave them the BOSH! treatment. Homemade mixed nut butter, melty chocolate, gooey dates—you're gonna *love* them.

Before you start: you will need a food processor. Line a large baking sheet with parchment paper. Preheat the oven to 375°F (190°C).

Toast nuts. Pour the nuts onto the lined baking sheet and spread out evenly. Toast the nuts in the preheated oven for 8–10 minutes, until light golden and fragrant (watch that they don't burn). Remove the sheet from the oven and let cool slightly for a few minutes.

Make nut butter. Transfer the nuts to a food processor while still warm and pulse, pausing occasionally to scrape down the sides, until you have a smooth, creamy nut butter—this can take up to 10 minutes (the nuts will turn from crumbs to a paste, then eventually into a nut butter). Add the sugar, if using, and salt and blend briefly to combine the seasonings into the nut butter. Set aside.

Melt chocolate. Break the chocolate into even-sized chunks, then place in a microwave-safe bowl and microwave in 20-second intervals, stirring each time, until melted and smooth.

Stuff dates. If the dates aren't already pitted, make a slit along the length of each one with a sharp knife and remove the pit. Fill each date with a teaspoon or two of the nut butter.

Coat dates. Working one at a time, dip one side of each date into the melted chocolate, letting any excess drip off into the bowl, and place the chocolate-coated date on the lined baking sheet. Sprinkle with a little extra salt, if you like. Repeat with the rest of the dates, then transfer the baking sheet to the fridge to set the chocolate.

Serve and store. Once set, the dates are ready to enjoy but will keep in an airtight container for up to 1 week. The stuffed dates can also be frozen for up to 3 months, stored in a freezer-safe container. Store any leftover nut butter in a jar in the fridge for up to 2 weeks.

TROPICAL GRANOLA BARS

PER PORTION:

- 6 PLANT POINTS
- 3g PROTEIN
- 216 kcal

Makes 12–16

3½oz (100g) pitted dates (about 6–8 Medjool dates or 12 smaller dates)
2 tbsp water
1¾oz (50g) dried mango
1¾oz (50g) dried pineapple
4 tbsp (60g) coconut oil
⅓ cup (100ml) maple (or agave) syrup
1 tsp vanilla extract
large pinch of sea salt
2¼ cups (200g) old-fashioned rolled oats
⅓ cup (30g) unsweetened shredded coconut
⅓ cup (50g) mixed seeds, such as pumpkin seeds, sunflower seeds and chia seeds
¼ cup (30g) chopped nuts, such as cashews or almonds

It's time you boshed a BOSH! bar! Packed with sunshine flavors and natural energy, these chewy, tropical bars are perfect for breakfast on-the-go, a lunch box treat, or a nourishing post-workout snack.

Before you start: you will need a food processor and a small saucepan. Line an 8in (20cm) square baking pan with parchment paper (or use rectangular silicone molds, about 4 x 1½ in/10 x 4 cm). Preheat the oven to 350°F (180°C).

Prep ingredients. Roughly chop the pitted dates and put them in a food processor with the 2 tablespoons water. Pulse to a sticky paste, adding more water, if needed—don't worry if it's not completely smooth. Chop the dried mango and pineapple into small pieces (about raisin-size).

Warm liquids. Melt the coconut oil in a small saucepan over low heat. Stir in the maple syrup, vanilla, and salt until combined. Turn off the heat but keep the pan on the stove to keep the mixture warm.

Combine mixture. Combine the dried fruits, oats, shredded coconut, mixed seeds, and chopped nuts in a large bowl. Pour the still-warm coconut oil mixture into the bowl, then add the date paste. Mix everything together thoroughly using a wooden spoon or your hands to ensure that all the dry ingredients are well combined—the mixture should hold together.

Bake bars. Pour the mixture into the lined baking pan (or silicone molds), pressing it down firmly and evenly with the back of a spoon. Bake in the preheated oven for 15–18 minutes (or 12–15 minutes if using the silicone molds), until the edges are just starting to turn golden brown. Remove from the oven and let cool and firm up.

Serve and store. Once cool and firm, turn the bake out of the pan (or molds) onto a cutting board, then cut into bars or squares with a sharp knife. Keep the granola bars in an airtight container for up to 1 week or freeze for up to 3 months, stored in a freezer-safe container.

COCONUT & CARDAMOM RICE PUDDING

PER PORTION:

- **3.25 PLANT POINTS**
- **3g PROTEIN**
- **271 kcal**

Serves 4

⅔ cup (120g) short-grain rice, such as pudding or Arborio
6 cardamom pods, lightly crushed (or ½ tsp ground cardamom), plus extra to serve
¾ cup (200g) coconut cream
2½ cups (600ml) coconut water
2–3 tbsp maple (or agave) syrup
pinch of sea salt

To serve
your choice of dried fruit
toasted coconut flakes
chia seeds

Rice pudding deserves a comeback; make this and you'll see why. Lusciously creamy, delicately spiced with cardamom and sweetened with coconut—it's cuddly comfort in a bowl.

Before you start: you will need a medium saucepan with lid.

Prep ingredients. Rinse the rice in a sieve under cold running water until the water runs clear, then drain. Lightly crush the cardamom pods (or measure out the ground cardamom).

Cook pudding. Add the rice, cardamom, coconut cream, coconut water, maple syrup, and salt to a medium saucepan over medium heat and bring to a simmer. Reduce the heat to low, cover with the lid, and simmer for 25–30 minutes, until the rice is tender, adding a little extra coconut water to loosen, if needed. Taste and adjust the seasoning with extra salt or sweetness, if needed.

Assemble and serve. Ladle the rice pudding into bowls and serve topped with your choice of dried fruit, coconut flakes, chia seeds, and an extra pinch of cardamom.

CHOCOLATE BANANA "CAKIES"

PER PORTION:
- **4.25 PLANT POINTS**
- **4g PROTEIN**
- **372 kcal**

Makes 6

3 ripe bananas
¼ cup(75g) coconut oil
1¾oz(50g) 70% plain chocolate
¼ cup(50g) coconut sugar
(or soft light brown sugar)
1 tsp vanilla extract or paste
⅓ cup (50g) raisins
1 tbsp chia seeds
1¼ cup (175g) all-purpose flour
1 tsp baking powder
½ tsp baking soda
1 tsp ground cinnamon
pinch of sea salt
2–3 tbsp plant-based milk

What do you get if you mix a cake with a cookie? A "cakie." Soft, chewy, chocolate-studded, and banana-loaded—these are unlike anything you've had before.

Before you start: you will need a small saucepan. Line a large baking sheet with parchment paper. Preheat the oven to 350°F (180°C).

Prep ingredients. Slice half of one of the bananas into 6 rounds and set aside. Mash the rest of the bananas in a large bowl with the back of a fork until smooth. Melt the coconut oil in a small saucepan over low heat. Roughly chop the chocolate into small pieces.

Make batter. Add the melted coconut oil, coconut sugar, vanilla, raisins, and chia seeds to the mashed bananas. Sift in the flour, baking powder, baking soda, cinnamon, and salt, and mix until combined. Fold in the plant-based milk until the mixture forms a cakelike batter; if it feels too stiff or dry, add a splash more plant-based milk to loosen.

Bake. Scoop 6 cookie-sized mounds of the batter onto the lined baking sheet, each about 2¼oz (70g). Press a slice of the reserved banana into the top of each one. Bake for 12 minutes, or until the edges are golden and the centers are set but still soft. Remove from the oven and cover the baking sheet with a clean, dry dish towel to keep the cakies soft, then let cool.

Serve and store. Enjoy these soft, cakelike banana cookies warm or at room temperature. Store in an airtight container for up to 2 days or freeze individually for up to 3 months.

PEAR, GINGER & BLUEBERRY CRUMBLE

PER PORTION:

- 4.75 PLANT POINTS
- 4g PROTEIN
- 381 kcal

Serves 6

For the crumble topping
2½oz (75g) coconut oil (or cold plant-based butter), plus extra for greasing
1 cup (90g) old-fashioned rolled oats
⅔ cup (75g) flour, preferably whole wheat
½ cup (75g) coconut sugar
1 tsp ground ginger
pinch of sea salt
¼ cup (30g) chopped nuts (almonds, pecans, and walnuts work well)

For the filling
4 ripe pears (but not overripe)
1 in (5 cm) piece of fresh ginger
3½oz (100g) blueberries
1 tbsp lemon juice
4 tbsp maple (or agave) syrup
½ tsp cornstarch

To serve
plant-based custard (or ice cream or crème fraîche)

Warming, sweet, and gently spiced, this fruity crumble is a perfect fall dessert. Pear and blueberry make a juicy, jammy base under a golden, nutty, ginger topping.

Before you start: you will need a large baking sheet. Lightly grease a medium baking dish. Preheat the oven to 350°F (180°C).

Start to prep crumble topping. Measure the coconut oil for the crumble and place in the fridge to harden. Measure out the remaining ingredients. Set aside.

Make filling. Peel, core, and dice the pears into bite-sized chunks. Peel and grate the ginger. Add the pears, blueberries, lemon juice, ginger, maple syrup, and cornstarch to a large bowl and mix well until everything is evenly combined. Transfer the fruit mixture to the greased baking dish and spread out evenly.

Mix crumble topping. In a separate bowl, mix together the oats, flour, sugar, ground ginger, and salt until combined. Add the cold coconut oil to the dry mix and use your fingers to rub it in until the mixture has a rough, crumbly texture with clumps. Stir in the nuts. Sprinkle the crumble topping evenly over the pear mixture.

Bake. Place the dish on a baking sheet and bake in the preheated oven for 30 minutes, until the top is golden brown and the fruit is bubbling at the edges. Let cool for 15 minutes before serving to allow the filling to thicken a little.

Assemble and serve. Spoon the crumble into serving bowls and enjoy warm with plant-based custard.

GINGER & BERRY BLACK BEAN BROWNIES

PER PORTION:

- 4.25 PLANT POINTS
- 3.5g PROTEIN
- 172 kcal

Serves 16

3¾oz (110g) crystallized ginger
3½oz (100g) 70% plain chocolate
1 cup(90g) old-fashioned rolled oats
large pinch of sea salt
½ cup (45g) cocoa powder
1 tsp baking powder
1 x 15oz (425g) can black beans
1 cup (240ml) plant-based milk
5 tbsp coconut oil, plus extra for greasing
⅓ cup (100g) maple (or agave) syrup
1 tbsp vanilla extract
2½oz(75g) blackberries

Brownies with benefits. These rich, fudgy bites are packed with protein and fiber. Their plain chocolaty flavor is lifted by warming ginger and bursts of juicy blackberry. Curious, but undeniably delicious.

Before you start: you will need a high-speed blender. Line the base of an 8in (20cm) square brownie pan with parchment paper, and grease the sides. Preheat the oven to 400°F (200°C).

Prep dry ingredients. Finely chop the crystallized ginger. Roughly chop the chocolate. Add the oats to a blender and blend to a powder. Pour the oats into a large mixing bowl. Sift the salt, cocoa powder, and baking powder into the bowl with the oats. Add in two-thirds of the crystallized ginger and all the chocolate.

Blend. Drain the black beans, rinse under cold running water, then drain again. Put the black beans, plant-based milk, coconut oil, syrup, and vanilla extract into the blender and blend to a smooth, runny consistency.

Make the batter. Add the blended black bean mixture to the oat mixture in the bowl and stir with a wooden spoon until well combined. Gently pour the batter into the prepared brownie pan, spread out evenly, and sprinkle the remaining ginger over. Gently press the blackberries evenly over the top.

Bake. Cook in the preheated oven for 20 minutes, until just set but still a little gooey in the middle. Let cool before cutting into squares.

Serve and store. Enjoy right away, or store the brownies for up to 4 days in an airtight container in the fridge. Alternatively, wrap individually and freeze in a freezer-safe container for up to 3 months.

MORE
PLAN
HACK

WHOLESOME HOT DRINKS

Ian has been drinking mushroom coffee for years and credits it with sustained energy and concentration levels throughout the day. Henry is very partial to a turmeric chai and enjoys one most evenings to wind down after a busy day.

MUSHROOM CACAO COFFEE

PER PORTION:

- **2.25 PLANT POINTS**
- **1g PROTEIN**
- **36 kcal**

Makes 20 servings

1½oz (40g) lion's mane mushroom powder
1oz (30g) cordyceps mushroom powder
1oz (30g) chaga mushroom powder
1oz (30g) ashwagandha powder
1oz (30g) maca root powder
¾oz (20g) rhodiola rosea powder
¾oz (20g) raw cacao powder
¾oz (20g) vitamin B5 powder
½oz (15g) good-quality instant coffee or caffeine powder
½oz (15g) sweetener of choice

Before you start: you will need a 1¾-cup (400ml) jar with lid.

Blend and store mix. Measure the powders into a bowl and mix until well combined. Spoon or pour the mixture through a funnel into a jar, and label it: "Super Mushroom Cacao Coffee:1 tablespoon = 1 cup."

Serve. Stir 1 tablespoon of the mushroom coffee into a mug containing 1 cup (200ml) just-boiled water or hot plant-based milk, or a mix of both. Sweeten to your preference, if you like.

GOLDEN TURMERIC CHAI

PER PORTION:

- **1.75 PLANT POINTS**
- **0g PROTEIN**
- **22 kcal**

Makes 20 servings

2oz (60g) coconut sugar
¾oz (20g) ground ginger
¾oz (20g) ground cardamom
¾oz (20g) ground cinnamon
¼oz (10g) ground turmeric
¼oz (10g) freshly ground black pepper
¼oz (10g) ground white pepper
1½ tsp ground cloves
pinch of ground nutmeg

Before you start: you will need a 1¼-cup (300ml) jar with lid.

Blend and store mix. Measure all the ingredients into a bowl and mix until well combined. Spoon or pour the mixture through a funnel into a jar, and label it: "Golden Turmeric Chai: 1 teaspoon = 1 cup."

Serve. Steep 1 teaspoon of the chai blend in a mug containing 1 cup (250ml) just-boiled water or hot plant-based milk, or a mix of both. Let infuse for 3–5 minutes, then either strain or enjoy right away.

ALL THE SUPER SEEDS

You'll have seen these peppered throughout the recipes in this book; they are an easy way to add a final flourish of flavor, crunch, and health benefits to your meals. These blends are rich in protein, fiber, omega-3 fatty acids, and essential minerals—great for supporting energy, digestion, and brain function. Sprinkle over salad, pasta, soup, or oats for a delicious whole-food boost.

PROTEIN PACKED

At BOSH! we're super keen on getting our protein in while focusing on whole foods. This seed blend is not only rich in protein, but it also provides magnesium, omega-3 fatty acids, and fiber. It's perfect to help you hit your daily protein target. Sprinkle over pasta, salads, oats, or anything else you fancy!

PER TBSP:

- **6.5 PLANT POINTS**
- **3.5g PLANT PROTEIN**
- **85 kcal**

Makes 1 medium jar

3 tbsp almonds
6 tbsp pumpkin seeds
4 tbsp sunflower seeds
2 tbsp hemp seeds
2 tbsp chia seeds
2 tbsp flaxseeds
3 tbsp nutritional yeast
½ tsp flaky sea salt
½ tsp freshly ground black pepper

Before you start: you will need a medium skillet and a medium jar.

Prep blend. Coarsely chop the almonds to roughly the same size as the pumpkin seeds. Heat a medium, dry skillet over medium heat until hot. Add the almonds, pumpkin seeds, and sunflower seeds. Toast for 2–3 minutes, tossing the pan occasionally, until the nuts/seeds are slightly golden and starting to pop. Add the hemp seeds, chia, and flaxseeds, and toast for a further 1–2 minutes until light golden.

Combine. Put the toasted nuts and seeds into a bowl, add the nutritional yeast, salt, and pepper, and stir well to combine. Set aside to cool.

Jar up and store. Transfer the cooled nut and seed blend to a jar, label, and put on the lid. Store in a cool place for up to 1 week or 3 months in the fridge. Use the mix to give salad, pasta, and oats more flavor and texture, as well as a nutritional boost.

BRAIN POWER

Walnuts and hemp, flax, and chia seeds are a good source of omega-3 fatty acids, which help support the brain and cognition. Pumpkin and sesame seeds provide zinc and magnesium, which can help reduce inflammation.

PER TBSP:
- **6.5 PLANT POINTS**
- **4.5g PROTEIN**
- **95 kcal**

Makes 1 medium jar

4 tbsp walnut halves
5 tbsp pumpkin seeds
4 tbsp hemp seeds
3 tbsp flaxseeds
2 tbsp chia seeds
2 tbsp sesame seeds
3 tbsp nutritional yeast
½ tsp flaky sea salt
½ tsp freshly ground black pepper

Before you start: you will need a medium skillet and a medium jar.

Prep blend. Coarsely chop the walnuts to roughly the same size as the pumpkin seeds. Heat a medium skillet over medium heat until hot. Add the walnuts and pumpkin seeds and toast for 2 minutes, until fragrant. Stir in the hemp, flax, chia, and sesame seeds and toast for a further minute or two until the seeds start to pop and their color deepens slightly.

Combine. Put the toasted nuts and seeds into a bowl, then stir in the nutritional yeast, salt, and pepper. Set aside to cool.

Jar up and store. Transfer to a jar, put on the lid, and label. Store in a cool place for up to 1 week, or for 3 months in the fridge. Use the mix to give breakfasts, salads, and dips more flavor and texture, as well as a nutritional boost.

GUT HEALTH

Chia, flax, and psyllium are a good source of soluble fiber, which promotes a healthy gut microbiome. Fennel aids digestion, and hemp, pumpkin, and sunflower seeds provide gut-supporting prebiotic minerals.

PER TBSP:
- **7.25 PLANT POINTS**
- **3.5g PROTEIN**
- **87 kcal**

Makes 1 medium jar

3 tbsp sunflower seeds
2 tbsp pumpkin seeds
5 tbsp chia seeds
4 tbsp flaxseeds
3 tbsp hemp seeds
2 tbsp fennel seeds
2 tbsp psyllium husk
½ tsp flaky sea salt
½ tsp freshly ground black pepper

Before you start: you will need a medium skillet and a medium jar.

Prep blend. Heat a medium, dry skillet over medium heat until hot. Add the sunflower and pumpkin seeds and toast for about 2 minutes, until lightly fragrant. Stir in the chia, flax, hemp, and fennel seeds, and toast for 1–2 minutes until the seeds begin to pop and their color deepens slightly.

Combine. Put the seeds into a bowl and let cool. Stir through the psyllium husk, salt, and pepper until combined.

Jar up and store. Transfer to a jar, put on the lid, and label. Store in a cool place for up to 1 week, or for 3 months in the fridge. Sprinkle over oats, yogurt, or salads for a daily fiber and prebiotic boost.

Gut health seed mix
Umami nooch
Spicy nooch
Protein-packed seed mix
Tingly nooch
Brain power seed mix
Zesty nooch

ALL THE NOOCH

Nooch (aka nutritional yeast) is savory, cheesy, and packed with B vitamins, and with added extras it becomes the ultimate flavor maker. These different nutritional yeast seasoning blends are made for upgrading proteins (like tofu and tempeh), roasted vegetables, pasta, popcorn, avocado toast, soups, scrambles, and more.

TINGLY

PER TBSP:
- **2 PLANT POINTS**
- **3g PROTEIN**
- **30 kcal**

Makes 9oz (250g)

3½oz (100g) nutritional yeast
1oz (25g) garlic granules or powder
1oz (25g) onion granules or powder
1oz (25g) ground Szechuan pepper
½oz (15g) fine sea salt
½oz (15g) gochugaru
¼oz (10g) mushroom powder, such as porcini or shiitake
¼oz (10g) paprika
¼oz (10g) food-grade citric acid (or finely grated zest of 2 unwaxed lemons; do not peel or the mix will become clumpy)
1 tsp ground white pepper
1 tsp freshly ground black pepper

Before you start: you will need a high-speed blender and a medium jar (or container) with lid.

Blend mix. Add all the ingredients to a blender and blend to a fine powder.

Jar up and store. Transfer the blend to a lidded jar or container and store for up to 1 month. Use in place of nutritional yeast for extra flavor and tingling heat from the Szechuan pepper.

UMAMI

PER TBSP:
- **1.75 PLANT POINTS**
- **4.5g PROTEIN**
- **39 kcal**

Makes 5½oz (150g)

3½oz (100g) nutritional yeast
½oz (15g) fine sea salt
1 tsp garlic granules or powder
1 tsp onion granules or powder
1 tsp mushroom powder, such as porcini or shiitake
1 tsp ground white pepper

Before you start: you will need a high-speed blender and a medium jar (or container) with lid.

Blend mix. Add all the ingredients to a blender and blend to a fine powder.

Jar up and store. Transfer the blend to a lidded jar or container and store for up to 1 month. Use in place of nutritional yeast in soups, stews, and sauces for added depth of flavor.

SPICY

PER TBSP:

- **2.5 PLANT POINTS**
- **3g PROTEIN**
- **33 kcal**

Makes 7oz (200g)

3½oz (100g) nutritional yeast
1oz (25g) sweet smoked paprika
¾oz (20g) mushroom powder, such as porcini or shiitake
½oz (15g) fine sea salt
½oz (15g) hot chili powder
¼oz (10g) food-grade citric acid (or finely grated zest of 2 unwaxed lemons; do not peel or the mix will become clumpy)
1 tsp ground white pepper
1 tsp ground ginger
1 tsp ground cumin
1 tsp ground cilantro
1 tsp ground fennel

Before you start: you will need a high-speed blender and a medium jar (or container) with lid.

Blend mix. Add all the ingredients to a blender and blend to a fine powder.

Jar up and store. Transfer the blend to a lidded jar or container and store for up to 1 month. Use in place of nutritional yeast for extra heat and savory flavor.

ZESTY

PER TBSP:

- **1.5 PLANT POINTS**
- **3g PROTEIN**
- **33 kcal**

Makes 7oz (200g)

3½oz (100g) nutritional yeast
1oz (25g) food-grade citric acid (or finely grated zest of 4 unwaxed lemons; do not peel or the mix will become clumpy)
¾oz (20g) onion granules or powder
¾oz (20g) garlic granules or powder
¾oz (20g) paprika
½oz (15g) fine sea salt
¼oz (10g) dried parsley

Before you start: you will need a high-speed blender and a medium jar (or container) with lid.

Blend mix. Add all the ingredients to a blender and blend to a fine powder.

Jar up and store. Transfer the blend to a lidded jar or container and store for up to 1 month. Use in place of nutritional yeast in pasta sauces, and salad dressings, or sprinkle over vegetables before roasting.

LONGEVITY BERRY MIX

PER PORTION:

- 6 PLANT POINTS
- 0.9g PROTEIN
- 41 kcal

Makes about 10 portions

10oz (300g) fresh or frozen blueberries
7oz (200g) fresh or frozen strawberries
5½oz (150g) fresh or frozen blackberries
5½oz (150g) fresh or frozen raspberries
3½oz (100g) fresh or frozen pomegranate seeds
3½oz (100g) fresh or frozen pitted cherries

A simple, nutrient-dense blend of berries and pomegranate seeds created to make smoothies, breakfasts, and desserts super quick and easy to make. Packed with antioxidants, fiber, and natural sweetness, this mix is perfect to keep on hand in the freezer. Just scoop and blend whenever you need a delicious, healthy boost.

Before you start: you will need a baking sheet and a large, sealable freezer bag or container (about 2 quarts/2 liters).

Prep ingredients. If using fresh fruit (if using frozen, skip this step), rinse gently, then pat dry with paper towels. Spread the fresh berries, pomegranate seeds, and cherries on a baking sheet in a single layer. Freeze for 2 hours, or until firm.

Combine fruit. Put the frozen fruit into a large bowl and toss lightly to distribute the different types, colors, and sizes evenly.

Store. Transfer the berry mix to a labeled, airtight freezer bag or container. Press out any excess air if needed, seal, and return to the freezer for easy scooping. It will keep for up to 3 months. Use the longevity berry mix to top breakfast bowls, desserts, or smoothies.

GREEN PLANT POINT CUBES

PER CUBE:

- 4 PLANT POINTS
- 2g PROTEIN
- 16 kcal per cube

Makes about 8 large cubes

14oz (400g) spinach leaves
1 tbsp chlorella
1 tbsp spirulina
1 tbsp moringa

A simple way to pack more plants into your day. Each cube is loaded with iron, chlorophyll, and plant power from spinach, chlorella, spirulina, and moringa. Add to smoothies, soups, stews, or sauces for a quick, healthy boost.

Before you start: you will need a high-speed blender and an extra-large ice-cube tray or mold.

Blend greens. Put the spinach in a blender, adding a tiny splash of water. Blend, adding a little extra water, if needed—be careful not to add too much or it will dilute the goodness. Once the spinach starts to break down, add the chlorella, spirulina, and moringa, then blend again to a thick paste.

Freeze and store. Spoon the spinach mixture into an ice-cube tray or mold, then freeze. To use the cubes, melt or blend into sauces, soups, stews, ragùs, or smoothies for an extra hit of goodness. Store for up to 3 months in the freezer.

ALL THE DRIZZLES

Condiments, reimagined. These delicious, creamy tofu drizzles are used to add the finishing touch to many of the recipes in this book. Not only do they lend color and flavor, but they're also a clever way of adding plant-rich protein to your meals.

FRESH GREEN DRIZZLE

PER BOTTLE:

- **2.75 PLANT POINTS**
- **51g PROTEIN**
- **453 kcal**

Makes 1 medium squeezy bottle

1 lime, plus extra, if needed
½ cup (25g) bunch of mint
½ cup (25g) bunch of cilantro
10oz (300g) silken tofu
pinch each of sea salt and freshly ground black pepper, plus extra to season

Before you start: you will need a high-speed blender and a medium squeezy bottle (or jar).

Prep drizzle. Juice the lime. Pick the mint and cilantro leaves from the stalks.

Blend drizzle. Add the lime juice, mint, and cilantro leaves, the silken tofu, salt, and pepper to a blender and blend until smooth. Taste and season with more salt, pepper, and lime juice, if needed.

Store. Transfer the drizzle to a squeezy bottle and store in the fridge for up to 5–7 days. Shake well before use.

ROMESCO DRIZZLE

PER BOTTLE:

- **4.5 PLANT POINTS**
- **65g PROTEIN**
- **874 kcal**

Makes 1 medium squeezy bottle

10oz (300g) silken tofu
3 red peppers from a jar
1¾oz (50g) roasted almonds
½ garlic clove
1 tbsp red wine vinegar, plus extra, if needed
1 tsp hot or sweet smoked paprika
sea salt and freshly ground black pepper

Before you start: you will need a high-speed blender and a medium squeezy bottle (or jar).

Blend drizzle. Add all the ingredients to a blender and blend until smooth. Taste and season with salt, pepper, or more vinegar, if needed.

Store. Transfer the drizzle to a squeezy bottle and store in the fridge for up to 5–7 days. Shake well before use.

PESTO DRIZZLE

PER BOTTLE:

- **4.75 PLANT POINTS**
- **76g PROTEIN**
- **923 kcal**

Makes 1 medium squeezy bottle

½ lemon
10oz (300g) silken tofu
½ cup (25g) basil leaves
3 tbsp pine nuts (or hazelnuts work well too)
½ garlic clove
3 tbsp nutritional yeast
sea salt and freshly ground black pepper

Before you start: you will need a high-speed blender and a medium squeezy bottle (or jar).

Blend drizzle. Squeeze the juice of ½ lemon into a blender. Add the rest of the ingredients and blend until smooth. Taste and season with salt, pepper, or more nutritional yeast, if needed.

Store. Transfer the drizzle to a squeezy bottle and store in the fridge for up to 5–7 days. Shake well before use.

ALL DAY RANCH DRIZZLE

PER BOTTLE:

- **2.5 PLANT POINTS**
- **64g PROTEIN**
- **563 kcal**

Makes 1 medium squeezy bottle

10oz (300g) silken tofu
⅓ cup (75ml) plant-based milk
2 tsp garlic granules or powder
2 tsp onion granules or powder
2 tsp dried dill
1 tsp dried chives
1 tsp American (or Dijon) mustard
1 tbsp white wine vinegar, plus extra if needed
sea salt and freshly ground black pepper

Before you start: you will need a high-speed blender and a medium squeezy bottle (or jar).

Blend drizzle. Add all the ingredients to a blender and blend until smooth. Taste and season with salt, pepper, and extra vinegar, if needed.

Store. Transfer the drizzle to a squeezy bottle and store in the fridge for up to 5–7 days. Shake well before use.

SUN-DRIED TOMATO DRIZZLE

PER BOTTLE:
- **2.5 PLANT POINTS**
- **52g PROTEIN**
- **748 kcal in total**

Makes 1 medium squeezy bottle

6–8 sun-dried tomatoes in oil
1 tbsp tomato paste
1 tsp sweet smoked paprika
2 tbsp oil from the jar of sun-dried tomatoes
1 tbsp balsamic vinegar
10oz (300g) silken tofu
1–2 tbsp warm water (optional depending on preferred thickness)
sea salt and freshly ground black pepper

Before you start: you will need a high-speed blender and a medium squeezy bottle (or jar).

Blend drizzle. Drain the sun-dried tomatoes and add to a blender with the rest of the ingredients. Blend until smooth, adding more warm water, if needed. Taste and season with salt and pepper.

Store. Transfer the drizzle to a squeezy bottle and store in the fridge for up to 5–7 days. Shake well before use.

SPICY KOREAN DRIZZLE

PER BOTTLE:
- **2.5 PLANT POINTS**
- **50g PROTEIN**
- **467 kcal in total**

Makes 1 medium squeezy bottle

1 lime
10oz (300g) silken tofu
1½ tbsp gochujang
1 tsp sriracha
2 tsp soy sauce
1 tsp maple (or agave) syrup
sea salt and freshly ground black pepper

Before you start: you will need a high-speed blender and a medium squeezy bottle (or jar).

Blend drizzle. Squeeze the juice of 1 lime into a blender. Add the remaining ingredients and blend until smooth. Taste and season with salt and pepper.

Store. Transfer the drizzle to a squeezy bottle and store in the fridge for up to 5–7 days. Shake well before use.

All day ranch drizzle
Sun-dried tomato drizzle
Romesco drizzle
Fresh green drizzle
Pesto drizzle
Spicy Korean drizzle

"MEATY" TOPPERS

These flavor-packed toppers are ideal for adding extra protein to your meals. They can be air-fried, baked, or pan-fried—simply choose the method that suits you best. Make a batch, keep in the fridge or freezer, and use to upgrade salads, grains, pasta, soups, or anything that needs a plant-based boost.

"BACON" BITS

PER PORTION:

- **1.25 PLANT POINTS**
- **23g PROTEIN**
- **268 kcal**

Serves 2

9½oz (280g) extra-firm tofu
1–2 tbsp olive oil
2 tsp liquid smoke
1 tbsp light soy sauce
1 tsp maple (or agave) syrup
small pinch of sea salt

Before you start: line a baking sheet with parchment paper (if using an oven). You will need a nonstick skillet (if cooking on a stove).

Prep tofu. Drain the tofu for 10 minutes and pat dry with paper towels to remove any excess moisture. Dice into ½ in (1 cm) cubes. Combine 1 tablespoon of the oil with the rest of the ingredients in a bowl. Add the tofu and mix well to coat.

Cook (pick one method):
Bake. Spread the tofu out on a lined baking sheet. Bake at 425°F (220°C) for 25–30 minutes, turning halfway, until golden and crisp.

Air fry. Add the tofu to a lined basket or tray. Air fry at 375°F (190°C) for 15–20 minutes, shaking or turning halfway, until golden and crisp.

Pan fry. Heat the remaining 1 tablespoon of olive oil in a nonstick skillet over medium-high heat. Add the tofu and cook for 8–10 minutes, stirring regularly, until golden and crisp.

Store. Keep for 1 week in the fridge or freeze for up to 3 months.

"CHICKEN" STRIPS

PER PORTION:

- **2.5 PLANT POINTS**
- **23g PROTEIN**
- **252 kcal**

Serves 2

9½oz (280g) extra-firm tofu
1–2 tbsp olive oil
1 tsp vegetable bouillon powder
½ tsp each garlic and onion powder
½ tsp onion powder
½ tsp each dried sage, rosemary, and thyme

Before you start: line a baking sheet with parchment paper (if using an oven). You will need a nonstick skillet (if cooking on a stove).

Prep tofu. Drain the tofu for 10 minutes and pat dry with kitchen towels to remove any excess moisture, then cut it in half lengthwise. Tear the tofu into ½ in (1cm) thick strips and pat dry again with more paper towels. Combine 1 tablespoon of the oil with the rest of the ingredients in a bowl, then add the tofu strips, and mix well to coat.

Cook (pick one method):
Bake. Spread the tofu out on a lined baking sheet. Bake at 425°F (220°C) for 25–30 minutes, turning halfway, until golden and beginning to crisp.

Air fry. Add the tofu to a lined basket or tray. Air fry at 375°F (190°C) for 12–15 minutes, shaking or turning halfway, until golden and beginning to crisp.

Pan fry. Heat the remaining 1 tablespoon of olive oil in a nonstick skillet over medium-high heat. Add the tofu and cook for 7–8 minutes, stirring regularly, until golden and beginning to crisp

Store. Keep for 1 week in the fridge or freeze for up to 3 months.

“CHORIZO” CRUMBLES

PER PORTION:

- 2.5 PLANT POINTS
- 23g PROTEIN
- 319 kcal

Serves 2

9½oz (280g) extra-firm tofu
2–3 tbsp olive oil
2 tsp sweet smoked paprika
1 tsp sweet paprika
1 tsp ground cumin
½ tsp ground cilantro
½ tsp ground fennel seeds (optional)
½ tsp chili flakes
1 tsp tomato paste
1 tbsp light soy sauce
1 tsp maple (or agave) syrup

Before you start: line a baking sheet with parchment paper (if using an oven). You will need a nonstick skillet (if cooking on a stove).

Prep tofu. Drain the tofu for 10 minutes and pat dry with paper towels to remove any excess moisture, then crumble into small chunks. Pat dry again with more paper towels. Combine 2 tablespoons of the oil with the spices, tomato paste, soy sauce, and maple syrup in a bowl. Add the tofu and mix well to coat.

Cook (pick one method):
Bake. Spread the tofu out on a lined baking sheet. Bake at 425°F (220°C) for 25 minutes, turning halfway, until golden and caramelized.

Air fry. Add the tofu to a lined basket or tray. Air fry at 375°F (190°C) for 12–15 minutes, shaking or turning halfway, until golden and caramelized.

Pan fry. Heat the remaining 1 tablespoon of olive oil in a nonstick skillet over medium-high heat. Add the tofu and cook for 8–10 minutes, stirring regularly, until golden and caramelized.

Store. Keep for 1 week in the fridge or freeze for up to 3 months.

"BEEFY" BITS

PER PORTION:

- **2.25 PLANT POINTS**
- **24g PROTEIN**
- **278 kcal**

Serves 2

9½oz (280g) extra-firm tofu
1–2 tbsp olive oil
1 tbsp dark soy sauce
1 tbsp nutritional yeast
2 tsp Marmite (or other yeast extract)
½ tsp freshly ground black pepper
½ tsp onion powder
pinch of hot smoked paprika

Before you start: line a baking sheet with parchment paper (if using an oven). You will need a nonstick skillet (if cooking on a stove).

Prep tofu. Drain the tofu for 10 minutes and pat dry with paper towels to remove any excess moisture, then crumble into small pieces. Combine 1 tablespoon of the olive oil with the soy sauce, nutritional yeast, Marmite, black pepper, onion powder, and smoked paprika in a bowl. Add the crumbled tofu and mix well to coat.

Cook (pick one method):
Bake. Spread the tofu out on a lined baking sheet. Bake at 425°F (220°C) for 25 minutes, turning once, until evenly browned.

Air fry. Add the tofu to a lined basket or tray. Air fry at 375°F (190°C) for 12–15 minutes, shaking or turning halfway, until golden and beginning to crisp.

Pan fry. Heat the remaining 1 tablespoon of olive oil in a nonstick skillet over medium–high heat. Add the tofu and cook for 7–8 minutes, stirring regularly, until deep golden brown.

Store. Keep for 1 week in the fridge or freeze for up to 3 months.

CRISPY TOFU

PER PORTION:

- 2.25 PLANT POINTS
- 23g PROTEIN
- 252 kcal

Serves 2

9½oz (280g) extra-firm tofu
1–2 tbsp olive oil
½ tsp onion powder
½ tsp garlic powder
½ tsp paprika
½ tsp fine sea salt
pinch of freshly ground black pepper

We developed this simple technique as a protein-rich alternative to crispy onions for curries. It's also a great way to add crunch to salads, bowls, soups, and more. All you need is a box grater and a few spices, then choose one of the cooking options, below. It keeps in the fridge for up to a week and freezes well, so it's always ready when you need it.

Before you start: line a baking sheet with parchment paper (if using an oven). You will need a nonstick skillet (if using a stove).

Prep tofu. Drain the tofu for 10 minutes and pat dry with paper towels to remove any excess moisture. Grate the tofu on the coarse side of a cheese grater. Add to a bowl along with 1 tablespoon of the olive oil, spices, salt, and pepper and turn until the tofu is coated in the seasonings.

Cook (pick one method):
Bake. Spread the tofu out on a lined baking sheet. Bake at 425°F (220°C) for 20–25 minutes, stirring halfway, until golden and crisp.

Air fry. Add the tofu to a lined basket or tray. Air fry at 375°F (190°C) for 10–15 minutes, shaking or turning halfway, until golden and crisp.

Pan fry. Heat the remaining 1 tablespoon of olive oil in a medium, nonstick skillet over a medium-high heat. Add the tofu and fry, stirring, for 10–15 minutes, until golden and crisp.

Store. Keep for 1 week in the fridge or freeze for up to 3 months.

ALL THE PICKLES

Your go-to guide for bright, punchy flavor on demand. From pink onions to crunchy cucumbers, these easy fridge pickles bring tang, texture, and gut-friendly goodness to almost any dish. Just follow the ratios and let time do its thing. Store in jars, keep chilled, and get ready to upgrade your burgers, bowls, tacos, and more!

Why pickle?
Pickling allows you to make the most of a surplus of fresh ingredients when they're at their peak. The fermentation process adds flavor and crunch along with health benefits like improved digestion, gut health, and enhanced bioavailability of nutrients. The science is straightforward: acidic vinegar, sugar, and salt work together to create an environment that prevents spoilage and unwanted bacterial growth, while creating a playground for flavor and beneficial bacteria.

Getting the balance right
Generally, a pickle contains a ratio of 3:2:1—3 parts vinegar to 2 parts water and 1 part sugar, with the addition of salt and sometimes spice. This balance of ingredients always works, so if in any doubt, stick to the tried-and-true 3:2:1! That said, you can play around with ratios to achieve different end results in terms of flavor and texture: more vinegar equals a more sour pickle; more sugar results in a sweeter pickle; while more water gives a more subtle pickle.

Pickling do's:

- Always use sterilized jars, ideally with a new lid (see box, below).
- For best results, use produce at its peak of freshness and in season.
- Heat the pickling liquid (vinegar, water, sugar, salt) until everything has dissolved.
- Depending on the type of pickle you're making, the pickling time can vary; always follow the recipe for the best results.
- Experiment with different flavorings, spices, and vinegars.
- Store your filled jars in the refrigerator until ready to use and refrigerate after opening

Pickling don'ts:

- Eye the ingredients—give them time to do their thing, and follow the timings in the recipe.
- Reuse the pickling liquid.
- Use unsterilized jars or dirty utensils.
- Reduce the acidity below 50 percent. For example, if using ⅓ cup (100ml) water, don't go below ¼ cup (50ml) vinegar.

How to sterilize jars

Always wash jars and lids in hot, soapy water and rinse thoroughly. Place them upright on a baking sheet in a preheated oven at 350°F (180°C) for 10–15 minutes, until dry. Alternatively, boil them in a large pot of water for 10 minutes, then carefully remove from the pan with tongs or oven gloves and let air dry. You can also sterilize jars in the dishwasher or microwave.

DILL PICKLES

PER 15g:
- **2.5 PLANT POINTS**
- **0g PROTEIN**
- **3 kcal**

Makes 1 quart (1 liter) jar

7 small cucumbers
2 garlic cloves
1 tbsp mustard seeds
¼ cup (10g) dill fronds

For the pickling liquid (1:1:1 vinegar/water/sugar)
1¼ cups (300ml) white wine vinegar
1¼ cups (300ml) water
1½ cups (300g) sugar
1½ tbsp (25g) fine salt

Before you start: you will need a small saucepan and a 1-quart (1-liter) sterilized jar (see p225).

Make pickling liquid. Add the vinegar, water, sugar, and salt to a small saucepan. Heat gently and stir until the sugar and salt dissolve. Remove from the heat and let cool slightly.

Prep vegetables. While the pickling liquid is cooling, wash the cucumbers, leave whole or slice in half or into spears. Peel and finely grate the garlic.

Pickle. Add the cucumbers, garlic, mustard seeds, and dill to the jar. Pour the pickling liquid over to submerge completely. Tap to remove any air bubbles and seal tightly with the lid.

Chill and store. Let cool, then chill for 12 hours before eating, or at least 48 hours to allow the dill to flavor everything. Keep the pickle for up to 1 month in the fridge.

PICKLED RED CABBAGE

PER 25g:
- **1.5 PLANT POINTS**
- **1g PROTEIN**
- **12 kcal**

Makes 1 quart (1 liter) jar

¼ red cabbage
1 tbsp caraway seeds
5 whole peppercorns

For the pickling liquid (8:8:1 vinegar/water/sugar)
1¾ cups (400ml) red wine vinegar
1¾ cups (400ml) water
¼ cup (50g) sugar
2 tsp fine salt

Before you start: you will need a small saucepan and a 1-quart (1-liter) sterilized jar (see p225).

Make the pickling liquid. Add the vinegar, water, sugar, and salt to a small saucepan. Heat gently and stir until the sugar and salt dissolve. Remove from the heat and let cool slightly.

Prep cabbage. While the pickling liquid is cooling, finely shred the red cabbage. Add to a bowl with the caraway seeds and peppercorns. Massage the cabbage gently with clean hands until it starts to soften.

Pickle. Pack the cabbage tightly into the jar. Pour the pickling liquid over to submerge completely. Tap to remove any air bubbles and seal tightly with the lid.

Chill and store. Let cool to room temperature, then chill for at least 1 hour before eating, although the pickle is best after 24 hours. Keep for up to 1 month in the fridge.

PICKLED JALAPEÑOS

PER CHILE:
- **1.5 PLANT POINTS**
- **0g PROTEIN**
- **8 kcal**

Makes 1 quart (1 liter) jar

20 jalapeño chiles
5 garlic cloves
1 tbsp cumin seeds

For the pickling liquid (3:2:1 vinegar/water/sugar)
2 cups (450ml) apple cider vinegar
1¼ cups (300ml) water
¾ cup (150g) sugar
¼ tsp (10g) fine salt

Before you start: you will need a small saucepan and a 1-quart (1-liter) sterilized jar (see p225).

Make the pickling liquid. Add the vinegar, water, sugar, and salt to a small saucepan. Heat gently and stir until the sugar and salt dissolve. Remove from the heat and let cool slightly.

Prepare vegetables. While the pickling liquid is cooling, thinly slice the jalapeños with a knife or mandoline and peel the garlic.

Pickle. Pack the jalapeños into the jar with the garlic and cumin seeds. Pour the warm pickling liquid over to submerge completely and seal tightly with the lid.

Chill and store. Let cool to room temperature, then chill for at least 1 hour before eating, although the pickle is best after 24 hours. Keep for up to 1 month in the fridge.

PINK PICKLED ONIONS

PER 25g:
- **1.5 PLANT POINTS**
- **0g PROTEIN**
- **7 kcal**

Makes 1 quart (1 liter) jar

4 red onions
5 whole peppercorns
1 bay leaf

For the pickling liquid (2:2:1 vinegar/water/sugar)
1¾ cups (400ml) white wine vinegar
1¾ cups (400ml) water
1 cup (200g) sugar
2 tsp fine salt

Before you start: you will need a small saucepan and a 1-quart (1-liter) sterilized jar (see p225).

Make the pickling liquid. Add the vinegar, sugar, and salt to a small saucepan. Heat gently and stir until the sugar and salt dissolve. Remove from the heat and let cool slightly.

Prep onions. While the pickling liquid is cooling, peel and thinly slice the onions.

Pickle. Pack the onions tightly into the jar with the peppercorns and bay leaf. Pour the warm pickling liquid over to submerge completely and seal tightly with the lid.

Chill and store. Let cool to room temperature, then chill for at least 1 hour before eating, although the pickle is best after 24 hours. Keep for up to 1 month in the fridge.

INDEX

A

B

C

D

E

F

G

S

T

U

V

W

Y

Z

ABOUT THE AUTHORS

From scrappy Sheffield beginnings to one of the biggest plant-based launches in UK retail history, childhood friends turned culinary trailblazers Henry Firth and Ian Theasby have never done things by halves. Since embarking on their plant-rich mission in 2016, they've driven a global movement with almost 5 billion views, millions of followers, and six *Sunday Times* bestsellers.

BOSH! is a culinary force and media powerhouse, delivering "Flavor for Life" through award-winning recipes, viral content, and crave-worthy creations. Their partnerships include Jaguar Land Rover through Eurest/Compass UK, P&O Cruises, and NHS Blood and Transplant, proving that vibrant taste and better choices belong everywhere.

Now they're hitting shelves nationwide with their boldest plant-rich retail rollout yet, making it easier and tastier than ever to put more plants on more plates.

ACKNOWLEDGMENTS

The book you're holding is the result of a lot of hard work from many talented people. It was a huge honor to work with every single one of them.

We're hugely grateful to our editorial director, Cara Armstrong, whose guidance has been invaluable, and to Lucy Sienkowska, our senior editor, for her sharp eye and calm advice. A big thank you to Jordan Lambley, our senior designer, for crafting such a beautiful book.

Our food team deserves a special mention. In particular, Craig Morrison (pictured), who put in an incredible amount of hard work and did a marvelous job, along with Hollie Plummer, Maisie Riddle, and Malena McQuarrie Gonzalez, who made sure that the recipes are truly book-worthy.

The recipes in this book came to life, thanks to the wonderful photography of Liz and Max Haarala Hamilton, the styling skills of Sam Dixon and Sonali Shah, and the support of assistant stylists Kristine Jakobsson and Sam Wong. Max Robinson selected the perfect props as stylist, while Luke Bird created the illustrations and our gorgeous, timeless cover.

Behind the scenes, we're grateful to Nicola Graimes for editing, John Friend for proofreading, and Vanessa Bird for indexing. Our consultant nutritionist, Fiona Hunter, compiled the nutritional data and checked the text for accuracy.

Thanks also to our barbers, Laurance at Charlie's on Fulham Palace Road and Jack at Neville's on Pont Street, and to our makeup artist, Kim Roy, for making sure we looked our best on shoot day.

Finally, a huge thanks to everyone else at DK who played a part in producing, marketing, and selling this book. We feel lucky to have worked with such a talented team.

Henry's family: thanks for all the love :-) I promise to keep you filled with tasty, nutritious goodness. Special thanks to Em-J and Berry for filling my evenings with fun. Moon and Stars x

Ian's family: thanks for everything. Your love and support mean the world.

Team BOSH!: you're the best team we could wish for. Thank you for all you do.

Our partners, past and present: thank you for helping us put more plants on plates.

Our associates and allies: thank you for your counsel, advice, and support.

Our friends: thank you for always being there.

Our followers: every like, comment, and share keeps this mission alive. We appreciate you all.

And finally, you: thank you for buying this book. We hope it helps you put more plants on your plate.

Henry **Craig** **Ian**

DK LONDON
Editorial Director Cara Armstrong
Senior Editor Lucy Sienkowska
US Senior Editor Jennette ElNaggar
Senior Designer Jordan Lambley
Production Editor Tony Phipps
Production Controller Kariss Ainsworth
Art Director Maxine Pedliham
Publishing Director Stephanie Jackson

DK DELHI
Project Editor Ankita Gupta
Senior Art Editor Ira Sharma
DTP Designer Satish Chandra Gaur
DTP Coordinator Pushpak Tyagi
Pre-production Manager Balwant Singh
Creative Head Malavika Talukder

Editorial Nicola Graimes
Design, Illustration, Cover Design Luke Bird

First American Edition, 2026
Published in the United States by DK Publishing,
a division of Penguin Random House LLC
1745 Broadway, 20th Floor, New York, NY 10019

26 27 28 29 30 10 9 8 7 6 5 4 3 2 1
001–355758–Mar/2026

Published in Great Britain by Dorling Kindersley Limited

ISBN 979-8-2171-3635-3

Printed and bound in China

www.dk.com

This book was made with Forest Stewardship Council™ certified paper—one small step in DK's commitment to a sustainable future.
Learn more at www.dk.com/uk/information/sustainability

Publisher's Acknowledgments
DK would like to thank Izzy Poulson for design assistance, John Friend for proofreading, Vanessa Bird for indexing, Fiona Hunter for nutritional consultancy, and Renee Wilmeth for consulting on the US edition.